Silas Weir Mitchell

Hephzibah Guinness

A draft on the bank of Spain

Silas Weir Mitchell

Hephzibah Guinness
A draft on the bank of Spain

ISBN/EAN: 9783743351745

Manufactured in Europe, USA, Canada, Australia, Japa

Cover: Foto ©ninafisch / pixelio.de

Manufactured and distributed by brebook publishing software (www.brebook.com)

Silas Weir Mitchell

Hephzibah Guinness

CONTENTS.

	PAGE
Hephzibah Guinness	5
Thee and You	97
A Draft on the Bank of Spain	171

HEPHZIBAH GUINNESS.

CHAPTER I.

On the fifteenth day of October, in the year 1807, a young man about the age of twenty walked slowly down Front Street in the quiet city of Philadelphia. The place was strange to him, and with the careless curiosity of youth he glanced about and enjoyed alike the freshness of the evening hour and the novelty of the scene.

To the lad—for he was hardly more—the air was delicious, because only the day before he had first set foot on shore after a wearisome ocean-voyage. All the afternoon a torrent of rain had fallen, but as he paused and looked westward at the corner of Cedar Street, the lessening rain, of which he had taken little heed, ceased of a sudden, and below the dun masses of swiftly-changing clouds the western sky became all aglow with yellow light, which set a rainbow over the broad Delaware and touched with gold the large drops of the ceasing shower.

The young man stood a moment gazing at the changeful sky, and then with a pleasant sense of sober contrast let his eyes wander over the broken roof-lines and broad gables of Front Street, noting how sombre the wetted brick houses became, and how black the shingled roofs with their patches of tufted green moss and smoother lichen. Then as he looked he saw, a few paces down the street, two superb buttonwoods from which the leaves were flitting fast, and his quick eye caught the mottled loveliness of their white and gray and green boles. Drawn by the unusual tints of these stately trunks, he turned southward, and walking towards them, stopped abruptly before the quaint house above which they spread their broad and gnarled branches.

The dwelling, of red and black-glazed bricks, set corner to corner, was what we still call a double house, having two windows on either side of a door, over which projected a peaked pent-house nearly hidden by scarlet masses of Virginia creeper, which also clung about the windows and the roof, and almost hid the chimneys. The house stood back from the street, and in front of it were two square grass-plots set round with low box borders. A paling fence, freshly whitewashed, bounded the little garden, and all about the house and its surroundings was an air of tranquil, easy comfort and well-bred dignity.

Along the whole line of Front Street—which was then the fashionable place of residence—the house-fronts were broken by white doorways with Doric pillars of wood, such as you may see to-day in certain city streets as you turn aside from the busy Strand in London. There were also many low Dutch stoops or porches, some roofed over and some uncovered, but few mansions as large and important as the house we have described.

As the rain ceased old men with their long pipes came out on the porches, and women's heads peeped from open windows to exchange bits of gossip, while up and down the pavements, as if this evening chat were an every-day thing, men of all classes wandered to take the air so soon as the fierce afternoon storm had spent its force.

As the young stranger moved along among sparse groups of gentlemen and others, he was struck with the variety of costume. The middle-aged and old adhered to the knee-breeches and buckles, the younger wore pantaloons of tight-fitting stocking-net, with shoes and silk stockings, or sometimes high boots with polished tops adorned with silk tassels. It was a pretty, picturesque street-scene, with its variety of puce-colored or dark velvet coats and ample cravats under scroll-brimmed beaver hats.

The sailor of 1807 dressed like the sailor of to-day, and the lad's figure would have seemed no more strange now than it did then. But a certain pride of carriage, broad shoulders set off by a loose jacket, and clothes tight on narrow hips, drew appreciative looks as he passed; and the eye which wandered upward must have dwelt pleased, I fancy, on the brown, handsome face, with its strong lines of forehead and a mouth of great sweetness above a somewhat over-large chin.

As the young man drew near to the buttonwoods a notable-looking person came with slow and thought-laden steps from the south. This gentleman was a man of six feet two or three inches, and of so large and manly a build that his great height was not observable. His face was largely modelled like his figure, and apart from his dress he looked better fitted to have ridden at the head of a regiment than to have dwelt amidst the quietness of early Philadelphia. The younger man saw, with the eye of one wont to take note of men's thews and sinews, the gigantic grace of the figure before him, and his curious glances slipped from the low, scroll-brimmed gray beaver hat to the straight-cut coat with its cloth buttons, and at last rested with approval on the plain shoes, devoid of buckle, and the ample gray calves above them.

As the drab giant turned to enter the gate of the house the young man followed him with his gaze, and a gleam of pleasure crossed his face as another of the persons in our little drama came into view. For as he looked the upper half of the house-door, on which was a heavy brass knocker, opened, and a woman of about thirty-five years, leaning on the upper edge of the lower half of the door, became suddenly aware of the tall Quaker coming up the walk. Resting her arms on the ledge, she looked out over the little space, and called aloud, quite briskly, "Marguerite! Marguerite!" Instantly from between the house and the garden-wall to the south of it came, as at the call of the prompter, yet another of our actors; and it was for her the young sailor stood still, like a dog on point.

The girl he saw was possibly sixteen years old, and was dressed in the plainest of Friends' attire, but as young people of that sect were rarely clad in those days, in a simple but costly gray silk gown, with the traditional folds of fine muslin about the throat, a plain silk kerchief pinned back on the shoulders, and a transparent cap closely drawn about the face. Under this cap was wicked splendor of hair, which might have been red, and had vicious ways of curling out here and there from the bondage of the cap, as if to see what the profane world was like. Within the sober boundaries of her Quaker head-gear was a face which prophetic nature meant should be of a stately beauty in years to come, but which just now was simply gracious with changing color and the tender loveliness which looks out on the world from the threshold of maturity.

At this moment a woman of middle age, in the most severe and accurate of Quaker dress, crossed the street, and catching the little garden-gate as it swung to behind the man, went in just after him. The resolute shelter of the Friends' bonnet hid the woman's face from all save those towards whom she turned it, or the young sailor might have seen it lower and grow hard; for as she went along the path of red gravel the young girl danced merrily up to the door at the call of the lady who stood within it. In her bosom the child had set a bunch of late moss roses, and over her cap and across her breast and around her waist had twined a string of the dark-red berries from which spring the scant calices of the sweetbrier and wild rose.

The woman in the doorway was fashionably clad in a short-waisted dark velvet dress, with tight-fitting sleeves ending at the upper forearm in a fall of rich lace. She wore her abundant black hair coiled on the back of her head, with little half curls on the forehead. The face below them was dark, sombre, and handsome, with an expression of sadness which rarely failed to impress painfully those who saw her for the first time. She smiled gravely and quietly as she saw the growing look of annoyance on the face of the Quakeress and the half-awed, half-amused expression on that of her young niece as she too caught a glance of reprobation.

"Good-evening, Mr. Guinness," she said. Most women of her class, who had been Friends, would have called the new-comer by his first name, but this woman, who had been bred a Quaker, but had early left their ranks for those of the Episcopal Church, set her face somewhat against Quaker manners, and in quitting their Society had totally left behind her all their ways and usages.

A sense of joy lit up the large features of the Friend as he answered, "Thou art well, I trust? and were I thee I would have my picture made as thou art now, in the frame of the doorway, with the door at the end of the entry open behind thee to make a square of gold out of the western sky. It was artfully devised, Elizabeth. As a Friend I am shocked at thee."

At this playful speech—during which he had taken her hand in greeting—Miss Howard's face took a half-amused, half-annoyed expression, which Arthur Guinness quickly comprehended as he heard a short cough behind him, and dropping Elizabeth's hand turned to see his sister Hephzibah, who was regarding with set, stern visage the scared child beside them.

Caught in the brilliant autumn jewelries she had gathered from the garden-wall, the girl, who knew well the hard face now turned upon her, at first caught up her treasures and was moved to fly, but on a sudden checked herself, and pausing drew up her pretty figure with a certain pride, and faced the enemy with a look half determined, half amused.

The stately aunt in the doorway fluttered her fan to and fro, and said, smiling, "Good-evening, Hephzibah. What is it ails you?"

"Nothing ails me," replied the Quakeress: "the ailment is here. It is the disease of the world's vanities in this child;" and turning to the girl she went on: "I had hoped that thou hadst learned to talk less and to laugh less; and, knowing well thy father's wishes, thou wouldst do better to avoid such gewgaws as these corals, which I suppose my friend Elizabeth hath unwisely tempted thee with."

The girl made a stern effort to check her mirth at her guardian's mistake, but Nature was too much mistress of this blithe playmate of hers, who suddenly broke into a riot of laughter, saying between her bursts of mirth, "Oh, but thou wilt pardon me, and thou knowest I never can help it—— Oh, thou knowest! and oh dear!" and so saying fled in despair to hide her irreverent mirth.

The Quakeress's face grew darker as she turned to Elizabeth. "Are these thy lessons?" she said.

"Good gracious!" said Miss Howard. "How utterly absurd! How could you make so droll a mistake? Those were not corals of the sea, but the jewels of our garden."

"It little matters," replied Hephzibah. "Thou art of our people no longer, and Friends' ways are not thy ways, and thou couldst not help but hurt us, even if thou wouldst not."

"And most surely I would not, as you ought to know by this time. Friends' ways are not my ways; and yet I have obeyed my good brother as to this child most straitly, even when—yes, even when I have thought it wrong to make so uncheerful a life for her, knowing well—oh, my God!—how sad and lonely it is to be through all the years to come." She said these words as she stood, still holding the open door and staring past the woman she addressed, as if she saw the long vista of time and the dark procession of those years of gloom.

Arthur looked wistfully into her eyes as he passed her and went into the house; and his sister, with a look of annoyance, said sharply, "I have other work to do;" and turning left them.

No word of all this came to the ears of the young sailor, but what he saw was as it were a pantomime. The girl with her rebel laughter; the stately Elizabeth Howard, whose air and dress and bearing brought some unbidden moisture to his eyes; the Quakeress; the stern, half-laughing giant in drab, —all helped to make up for him a little drama within the white palings.

"*Comme c'est drôle!*" he murmured. "*Qu'elle est belle la Marguerite!*" and so saying turned and went lazily southward down Front Street, glancing around as he went as if looking for some one whose coming he expected. Musing over the chances which had left him landless, homeless, and moneyless, the young Frenchman strode along gayly, still keeping a lookout for his friend. As he passed Christian Street and the houses grew scarce, he saw coming towards him the person whom he sought. The new-comer was a man of middle age, dressed somewhat carefully in rather worn black clothes with patched black silk stockings, and low shoes with silver buckles. The style of costume, especially the rounded low beaver hat with the rim scrolled upwards in triple rolls, marked the owner for an emigrant abbé,—a figure and character which had become familiar enough in Philadelphia, where the French Revolution had stranded numberless unhappy waifs of all classes.

The abbé was a pleasant-looking man of rather delicate features and build, but somewhat ruddy for so slight a person. A certain erectness of carriage was possibly the inheritance by middle life of a youth spent in camps, and around the mouth some traitor lines bespoke love of ease and good living, and gave reason to guess why he had found it pleasant to abandon his regiment for the charming convent which looked downward over Divonne upon the distant Lake of Geneva, and across miles of walnut-groves and tangled vineyards which clothe the slopes of the purple Jura.

"Good-evening," said the younger man: "you are the welcome."

The abbé laughed. "If you *will* speak English,"

he said, in accents which but slightly betrayed his birth, as indeed they did rarely save in moments of excitement—" if you *will* speak English, say, ' You are welcome.' "

"Ah, but it is that I find it difficult," returned the sailor; "and how strange is all the land we have here!"

"All lands seem strange to the young," said the abbé, "but to me none are strange; and all are much the same, because no climate disagrees with all wines or with cards, and at forty one is at least a little *philosophe*. It seems a tranquil town, and what they call comfortable."

"At the least," answered the other, "we shall find here a safe home, and, as I trust, something to keep to us the morsel of bread, until better times arrive to our dear France. I have given my letters, and I have hope to get me a place in the bureau of this Monsieur Guinness. It will seem strange at first."

"Not less than to me to teach these young misses to talk the tongue of France," said the abbé.

"I have seen one this evening," returned the sailor, "which I should find pleasing to teach."

"Ah, you find them pretty?" said the abbé. "Better, *cher baron*, to forget the *beau sexe:* we are not of Versailles to-day."

"You should remember, in turn," answered his nephew, "that I am here only M. de Vismes; we are barons no longer."

"You have reason, Henri," said the elder man. "It is like those little comedies we used to play at the Trianon. And, *ma foi!* here I saw but yesterday

M. le Comte de St. Pierre teaching to dance, as I saw him once in that charming little play—— How one's memory fails! What was it, Henri? But no matter; all life is to act. Ah, I think that has been said before. How stupid to say what already has been said! But alas for our grandchildren! it will be for them impossible to say something new."

"What difference?" laughed the younger man. "There are things which to say and to hear shall be pleasant always;" and the lad kept silence, thinking of the little nothings his mother had said to him, a child, when, hand in hand, they wandered beside the braided streamlets of Divonne.

Meanwhile the abbé chatted of camp and court, until at last, as they strolled along, lonely men, past the open windows and crowded steps,—for the evening was warm,—the younger exclaimed, "Here, some place, I ought to find the house of Monsieur Guinness, which I was to see to-night. Is it already too soon?"

"Ah, not, I think; but we may wait yet a little, and return again."

"And this is it," said the younger, pausing.

The house was a plain brick dwelling, with the usual wooden Doric pillars, painted white.

Marking the place, the two Frenchmen strolled away up Front Street, to return somewhat later in the evening. They fell into silence as they walked, and the elder man amused himself with a vague kind of wonder at the *caractère sérieux* and *tout à fait Anglais* of his nephew, little dreaming that the young man was in like fashion marvelling that through camp and court and cloister, and sad prisons and in awful nearness of death on the scaffold, his uncle should have kept his gay, careless, sceptical nature, his capacity to find some trivial pleasure in all things. He could not understand how a man who had been so close to death in many shapes should yet have brought away with him no shadow of its sombre fellowship, and should have learned only to disbelieve and to doubt. He himself, beneath the natural childlike joyousness of his race which made hardships light, concealed for use in darker hours a firm will and a sober steadiness of moral balance, which perhaps came to him from his English mother, and dowered him with a manhood planned for upright, honorable pursuit of noble purposes,—a sweet, grave, earnest nature, with the even sunny temper of a sunny day.

CHAPTER II.

INTO the parlor of the house they had just passed came a few minutes later a tall, gaunt, angular woman, whose stiff and bony outlines were made mercilessly evident by a closely-fitting drab dress with tight plain sleeves and the studiously simple muslin worn only by rigid Friends. Her face was colorless like her dress; her hair, almost a perfect white, was worn flat under her cap; her features were large and not lacking in a certain nobleness of outline, but strangely wanting in any expression save that of severe and steady self-control. The room was square, and plainly panelled in white-painted pine; the furniture throughout of rigid, upright mahogany, with black hair-cloth seats to the chairs. On a claw-toed table double silver candelabra with wax candles would have but dimly lighted the room had it not been for the ruddy glow of a hickory-wood fire which flashed across large, brightly-polished andirons and a brass fender cut into delicate open-work. The walls were white; the floor was without carpet, and sanded in curious figures.

Miss Hephzibah Guinness paused as she entered the room and looked critically about her. Then she snuffed the candles and rang a small silver bell which stood on the table. Presently appeared a little black maid, clad much like her mistress, but in rather less accurate fashion. Mistress Hephzibah pointed sternly to a corner of the room where an active spider had spread his net.

The little maid examined it curiously: "Done made it sence dis mornin'."

"And this also?" said the lady, indicating a place on the floor where the carefully-made figures traced by sifting the sand out of a colander were incomplete. "Thou shouldst have been as careful as the spider. Consider his work,—how neat, Dorcas."

"Couldn't consider dat, missus, ef I had a-sp'iled him wid de brush."

The face of the mistress showed no signs of amusement at this ready retort. "Brush away the web," she said, "and keep thy thoughts to thyself."

The little maid bestirred herself briskly under the grave eye of her mistress, and presently the knocker was heard.

"Thy master is out," said Hephzibah, "but I will see any one who may call."

In a moment or two the maid came back. "Two gentlemen to see the master," said the girl.

"And thou hast left them to stand in the entry! Bid them come in at once."

A moment later the Abbé de Vismes and his nephew entered the room. The younger man cast a glance of amused curiosity at the apartment and at its sombre occupant, who advanced to meet them. The abbé bowed profoundly, without showing a trace of the amazement he felt at this novel interior and the tall and serious figure before him. "Allow me," he said, "to present myself: I am the Abbé de Vismes, and this is my nephew, Monsieur de Vismes. We have an appointment with Monsieur Guinness. Have I the great pleasure to see his wife?"

"I am his sister," said Hephzibah, shortly. As he named himself a shudder passed over her, and she steadied herself by seizing the back of a chair as she thought, "Alas! is the bitter bread coming back on the waters?" Then she recovered her control with an effort, and added, aloud, "My brother is not married. Take seats, friends."

"Ah," exclaimed the baron to himself, "what a droll country! *Elle le tutoie.* It must be a fashion of Quakre."

"I should well have known you for the sister," said the abbé: "the likeness is plain to see;" and this was true. He had seen the brother, and was struck now with the resemblance of features and the unlikeness of expression.

"It hath been spoken of by many," she said, replying to his remark. "My brother will be in by and by. You must be, I think, of the unhappy ones who have been cast on our shores by the sad warfare in France?"

"We are indeed unfortunate émigrés," returned the abbé, "who have brought letters from friends of your brother."

"From France?" she exclaimed, hastily.

"No; ah, no," he answered; "from England."

"And," she said, with a sense of relief, "and— and you do not know any one here?"

"We have that ill-fortune," he returned, "but hope soon to make friends. As yet it is all most strange to us, and as poverty is a dear tailor, I might ask that we be excused to present ourselves in a dress so unfit. My nephew came a sailor, and the dress he has not yet found time to alter."

The woman's changeless face turned toward the lad and met his ready smile, and she had in her heart a new pang, because she bethought her, "Had I been a wife and mother, the son I might have had would have been like this lad smiling at me to-day." But the answer she made was like many answers,— the thought least near to her heart: "The young man's apparel is well for his way of life, and hath the value of fitness. But perhaps thou dost not know that we of the Society of Friends observe a certain plainness of dress ourselves, and are for this reason but little apt to criticise the dress which is plain because of wear or poverty?"

"Without doubt, then," laughed the abbé, glancing down at his shining breeches and well-darned hose, "I should pass well the trial. They are all grown to a pleasant likeness of tint by reason that they have shared like trials of sun and rain, and, *mon Dieu!* they are as well worn as my conscience."

Hephzibah turned upon him with a real sense of shock, and as one wont in meeting to obey the impulse of speech when it grew strong, she said, "I understand not thy language,—indeed, almost none of it,—but yet enough to know thou hast spoken as lightly of the great Maker as unwisely of the friend we call conscience. Do I rightly suppose thee to be a minister among thy people?"

The lad ceased smiling as he saw her graver face, and the abbé, profoundly puzzled at the sermon his slight text had brought out, and yet seeing he had made a false step, said, "Alas! I have been so long away from my flock that I am forgetting the simple tongue of the shepherd."

The woman did not see the amused twinkle in the eye of this gay shepherd of the joyous Trianon, and missed too the sudden glance of amazement in the face of the nephew. She was engaged, as always, in an abrupt, suspicious study of her own motives in speaking, and would have wished to be silent a while. But there was need to speak, and therefore she said, "I am an unfit vessel for the bearing of reproach to another, but thy words startled me, and the thought

I was thinking spoke itself. Thou wilt consider kindly my saying."

The abbé was somewhat bewildered at the English used, but he said, "The fair sex hath its privileges to speak what it will, madame: it is ours to obey."

Hephzibah disliked the gay answer, and turning to the young sailor said, "Thou hast come to shore in our pleasant October weather. Has it its like in France?"

"Ah me!" he answered, "they gather the vintage these days on the slopes of the Jura, and the sun is less warm than ours, and—— Pardon, I like it here." He paused, with a choking in his throat as he remembered the yellowing walnut groves and the gray château of Dex and the distant sapphire lake.

Hephzibah's face softened anew. "It is hard," she said, "to leave friends and home, but this is perhaps a way, among many, to soften the hearts which are grown hard. And He has many ways to touch us—many ways," she added musingly, for she was thinking of what a soul-quake had shaken her own being at the sound of a name unheard for years.

"Ah, madame," he said, "my heart is not hard, and the world seemed so sweet to me once, when all those that I loved did live."

"But perchance they died that thou mightst more truly live," said Hephzibah, in calm technical tones.

"Then I would be dead rather," said young De Vismes fiercely, puzzled and hurt.

"Ah me!" said the abbé. "You have well said, madame. When that we are gone past many troubles it is that we learn to live. Let us make haste to enjoy the sun and the wine and the pleasant things, as the wise Solomon has bidden us."

"But that is so little of life!" said his nephew, sadly.

"And I fear," added Hephzibah, sternly, "that we are as them that speak to one another in strange tongues, not understanding. But here comes my brother."

As she spoke Arthur Guinness entered the room, wearing his hat after the fashion of Friends. "These," said his sister, "be friends which have come to thee, Arthur, with letters from thy correspondents in England."

"They are welcome," said he. "I am glad to see thee again; and this must be the nephew of whom thou hast spoken, and whose letters I have had."

"Yes," said the abbé,—"my nephew the Baron de Vismes."

Arthur Guinness took the lad's hand, smiling, and saying, "Well, if he is to be one of my young men, it will be best that he lay aside his title, and his name is—— Yes, I remember in my letter,—it is Henry. He shall be for us plain Henry, after the manner of Friends."

Then his sister excused herself and went out, leaving them to discuss the lad's future. As she climbed the stairs her limbs became weak, and, her features relaxing, her face too grew weary. "What have I done," she said, "wherein I took not counsel with the Spirit? These are thoughts which bring madness: I will not harbor them. It must have been done wisely." So she stood a moment before the tall old Wagstaffe clock which faced her at the head of the stairs ticking solemnly. Then she gathered up her strength, saying, "Yet a little while, a little while! Why dost thou mock me with the memory of a doubtful hour?" and then went on to her chamber in silence. Twice as she moved along the dark, cold entry, hearing the busy ticking close behind her,—twice she turned resolutely, with a feeling as if the tall old coffin-like clerk of Time were pursuing her steps.

As she closed the door of her chamber she heard with a shiver the ample ringing tones of her brother's voice. It was for her just then a sound of horror. Why, she did not pause to ask herself: perhaps because its wholesome pleasantness was in too sharp contrast with her new misery,—perhaps because it brought before her, in the possible form of a severe judge, the man she loved and honored, and also feared the most. Theirs were richly-contrasted natures,—each a compound of what Nature and a creed had made; for earnestly-believing people are themselves and a creed, or a creed and themselves,—and she was a creed and herself,—and he was himself above all and a creed.

Arthur Guinness was saying cheerily, "Will you come up to my study? We smoke no pipes in my sister's room, because it pleases her not, and—— Well, in my room here it will be no offence to the tender-minded among Friends who may chance to come, and who like not such vanities."

"We shall have pleasure to smoke with you," said the abbé, following him.

At the head of the first flight of stairs Arthur

Guinness passed with his guests into a room in the second story of what all Philadelphians know as the "back buildings,"—an arrangement which in later years caused a witty New Yorker to say that Philadelphians built their houses like frying-pans, and lived in the handles.

The room was sanded, like the parlor, but was filled with books, and on the table were pipes with long reed stems, a tobacco-pot, and two handsome silver tankards with arms engraved upon them. Above the fire was a genealogical tree of the Guinness family, for, like many Friends even to this day, Arthur Guinness took a certain half-concealed pride in an honorable descent from ancient Kentish stock, and valued himself more than he cared to state on his store of heavy plate.

The abbé's eye took in with approval the sober luxury and air of culture as they sat down to their pipes, while their host went on to say, "Well, then, it shall be so arranged: the lad comes to my counting-house; and if thou art still of the same mind on Third day—which is to-morrow—I will go with thee to Elizabeth Howard, who, I doubt not, will be pleased to have thee instruct her niece in the tongue of France. I see no need myself that a child of Friends should learn these foreign tongues, but as her guardian I have been somewhat careful not to insist too much on my own views."

"I shall find it a pleasant task, no doubt," said the abbé; "and might I ask that you will also do my nephew the honor to present him to Miss Howard, or such other of your friends as may make it pleasant for the lad? I fear he may find it *triste* in this new land."

Arthur Guinness hesitated: "Yes, yes, by and by. But thou wilt pardon me if I ask that I be excused from presenting him where there are only women. Friend Elizabeth hath some strong notions as to the bringing up of the child, and she does not wish that she should have acquaintances among young men. It is a fancy, but——"

"Nay, but pardon me," said the abbé. "I meant not to ask anything unusual, and no doubt in time he will find friends."

"Yes, yes," said Guinness. "Women have their ways,—women have their ways; but I was not sorry to mention this, because thou wilt be sure to like her, and what more natural than some time to ask leave to take with thee my young friend here? She would without doubt say no, and I may spare thee annoyance."

The abbé thought this frank speech strange enough, and young De Vismes, who listened quietly, felt an odd sense of disappointment; but both made haste to turn the chat aside, and under a cloud of smoke they talked the evening away pleasantly enough.

As they parted at the door Arthur said, laughingly, "Thou wilt pardon, I am sure, what I have said of my friend Elizabeth Howard. She hath but this one strangeness, and in all else thou wilt find her a woman of noble ways and a great fulness of fresh and pleasant life."

The abbé made a courteous reply, and the two strangers went away somewhat easier in mind.

CHAPTER III.

On the morning of the following day, Miss—or, as it was the usage then to say of middle-aged, unmarried women, Mistress—Elizabeth Howard sat at the window of her house near the corner of Front and Shippen Streets. The day was one of those soft, still October gifts when the sun seems warm again, and the winds stir not, and leaves cease to fall, and the changing year appears to relent and linger, and the southward-flitting robin loiters, cheated for a day. The woman sat quietly in the open window, a stately and, to the least observant, a remarkable-looking person. She was in early middle life, possibly thirty-five. The outline of her face was of the Roman type, delicate in the detail of the light proud nostril, and bold and noble in the general contour of feature. The mouth was a little large, but clearly cut, the chin full and decided. Over a forehead rather high, and more strongly moulded than is common in women, clustered plentiful black hair, curled short in the fashion then oddly called Brutus. A skin of smooth dark rich nectarine bloom made soft the lines of this face, which in repose was at times somewhat stern. The more acute observer would have been struck with the sombre, thoughtful air of command and power in the brow, the mysterious sweetness of the dark-gray eyes, and the contradictory lines of mirth and humor about the mouth.

Nature had here formed a remarkable character, and circumstance had given it a strange part to play in the drama of life.

In the garden in front of her and below the window, a charming contrast, sat her niece Marguerite, not less a contrast in her plainest of Friends' dress than in the blonde beauty of her young and fast-ripening form.

Presently the large blue eyes ceased wandering from the book on her lap to the mottled buttonwood bole or the forms of passing wayfarers seen between the snowdrop-bushes. "I promised my guardian to read it," she said; and the blue eyes turned up to meet the friendly gaze above her. "But I do not like the man in the book. Thee could not read it: thee would never have liked Friend Fox."

"A nice Quaker you are!" said her aunt, laughing. "Say thou, thou, or you will never learn to speak in meeting."

"I never want to," cried the girl, pouting. "I like bright things,—red things, blue things. I was never meant to be a Quaker. Why may I not go to Christ Church with thee, and wear gay clothes like the trees, aunty? They had no Fox. I wonder Master Penn did not run away when he saw the red hickories and the yellow maples. I will not read it;" and so saying she threw the book on the grass, and throwing a kiss to her aunt began to pluck the bright autumn flowers at her feet.

"The way was set for you by another will than mine," said her aunt. "Be content to walk in it, Marguerite. Perhaps it is better as it is."

"Perhaps," said the girl,—"yes, perhaps; but when I am twenty-one there will be no 'perhaps.'"

"You will always respect the wish of your dead father," said Miss Howard.

The girl looked grave, the elder woman troubled.

"Is Marguerite a Friend's name?" said her niece, pausing and facing her.

"No," returned her aunt. "You know well, my dear, that your mother was a Frenchwoman, and that you bear her name."

"And was she of our Society, aunt?" said the girl. "I wish I could have seen her."

"I wish you could," said the elder woman, ignoring the question. "Ah, I must hasten to ask Hephzibah to make you a better Quaker. I am a poor teacher, I think. I should begin by dyeing those big blue eyes gray, and painting those red cheeks white, as Hephzibah did her brass clock last year;" and the two laughed merrily at the remembrance.

"I did not tell you," said the elder, "that I had a note this morning telling me that we are to have the honor to-day of a visit from a committee of Friends. It cannot be for me, and I suppose it is about some of your madcap pranks."

"Oh, not for me, surely!" said the girl, a little scared. "That must be Hephzibah Guinness's doings. I hate her!"

"Hush!" said her aunt, smiling. "Here she comes. Get thee gone, little scamp!"

"Of a verity, the Spirit persuadeth me to depart," said the girl under her breath; and hastily gathering her flowers in her lap she fled around the corner of the house, dropping asters, Queen Margarets, and autumn leaves here and there as she went.

Her aunt rose from her seat and went across the room to the entry to open the door. "My task is too hard," she said,—"too hard. The past is so black, and the future so dark; and, ah me! I am so made that to-day is sunny always. How can life be pleasant to me? I wonder at myself. Come in, Hephzibah;" and so saying she took the hand of the new-comer, and the two entered the parlor.

It was a room of another kind from that which Hephzibah had left, and under her Quaker bonnet the thin, gaunt face darkened grimly as she looked about her. She had been there a hundred times before, but to-day, as always, it shocked her that any one should think needful the luxury and color with which Elizabeth Howard delighted to surround herself. The two women were as much apart as their creeds or their social surroundings; and as I see them now in that far-away time, in the wainscoted parlor, they are to me sharp and vivid pictures. In a high-backed chair of exquisitely carved dark mahogany sat the handsome, richly-clad lady, one shapely foot on the shining brass fender which fenced in a lazy wood-fire. A large feather fan guarded her face from the blaze, and, when she pleased, from the keen gaze of Hephzibah Guinness, whose stiff gray pent-house bonnet did her a like service at times, since the least turn of the head served to hide her face from view.

These two women were made by Nature to dislike and respect one another, and sometimes the dislike was uppermost, and sometimes the respect. The chances of life had thrown them together, since Marguerite Howard was the ward of Arthur Guinness and his sister, and destined by her father's will to be educated in the straitest ways of Friends. The male guardian had come by degrees to concede to his sister all such minor details as concerned the girl's dress and manners. And to this strange and implacable overseeing on the part of the Quakeress, Elizabeth Howard also had yielded after many inward and some outward struggles. She knew that to be a Friend was for years, at least, the child's fate, and once having submitted as to the main question, she felt that rebellion in lesser matters was unwise, and also unfair to the memory of the brother who had thus ordered his child's life. At times Miss Howard rebelled, but chiefly because she did not dislike a skirmish with Hephzibah Guinness, and because her sense of humor was so ungovernably strong as to break out despite her better judgment when things done or ordered by the Quaker guardians struck her as amusing.

On the other hand, Hephzibah was a little afraid of Miss Howard's merciless capacity for ridicule, but was quite as ready as she to cross swords in defence of her own views, which, owing to her narrow, well-fenced-in life, she had come to regard with the entire respect which some people entertain for their own opinions. Indeed, could Hephzibah Guinness have blotted out one doubtful act of her life, it is probable that she would have regarded herself with the most absolute approbation.

Elizabeth Howard was not to-day in the best of humors, owing chiefly to the curt note which told her of the visit of a committee of Friends,—an incident of which she had already some previous and not very agreeable remembrances. She began in Friends' language, which she used but rarely, and never to Arthur Guinness, for whom she was surely and always her noble natural self. "Wilt thou not take off thy bonnet, Hephzibah?" she said: "the room is warm."

"No," answered Hephzibah, absently; "I am not warm."

Then the bonnet itself struck Miss Howard suddenly in an absurd point of view, as everything good or bad did at some time. "How convenient," she added, "thy bonnet must have been to thee in thy younger days!"

"Why?" said Hephzibah, shortly.

"Well, my dear, no man could see you were looking at him; and it's such a nice hiding-place: a fan is a trifle to it."

"I had other and wiser occupation in my youth," said Hephzibah, "than to observe young men. But I have noticed that nothing is too serious to escape thy tendency to ridicule."

"Bless me!" returned Miss Howard: "is a Quaker bonnet a kind of saint's halo? I see nothing serious in it except your face, Hephzibah, which is serious enough."

"How is Margaret?" said Hephzibah, abruptly.

"As usual," said the other, feeling with a sense of comfort that her rapier had gone home. "Will you see her?"

"No," said the Quakeress. "I would speak with thee of a matter about one of my friends, if only thou canst put away thy mirth for a time and consider gravely the thing I would say."

"Now, my dear," laughed Miss Howard, "I shall be as serenely judicious as the clerk of Fourth Street meeting. But have you not known me well enough and long enough to be sure that if I do not get my every-day supply of laughter I must die?"

"Thou speakest lightly of dying," returned Hephzibah.

"And why not?" said the other. "I do not know the thing on earth so grim or grave that some time it has not a mirthful look. Some people cry and love and cry and pray. I believe there are people who can smile at their prayers and yet pray as well. Let us live our lives honestly. I should laugh at a jest if I were dying,—ay, and fear not that God would frown. What is it I can do for you, Hephzibah?"

The Quakeress hesitated a moment, but Miss Howard's last phrase was spoken kindly and gently. "I have a—a friend," said Hephzibah, halting a little at the unusual task of equivocation. "I have a friend to whom came many years ago a chance to turn the whole life of a young person from the vanity of worldly ways and the teachings of a hireling ministry by hiding—no, by not telling—something which she knew. The concealment hurt no one, and saved a life from the vain ways of the world."

"Well?" said Elizabeth, in utter amazement at the nature of the statement set before her.

"I think well," went on Hephzibah, "of thy judgment, even when warped by the errors of the world. Wouldst thou not have done the like?"

"I?" said Elizabeth, proudly,—"I? You may well ask me what I *think* of it,—of such a thing; but to ask me if I would *do* it! How can you cheat a soul into righteousness? This comes of a creed which can never see beyond its own gray horizon. How could you dare to ask me such a question?" And so saying the woman rose and stood by the fire, looking down on the moveless visage of Hephzibah. She was a woman with a sense of honor found rarely enough among men, and this thing stirred her as an insult disturbs a man.

Meanwhile, Hephzibah repented somewhat her design to fortify her resolution by the idea of what another woman whom she respected might think of her action. "I think," she said, "thou hast perhaps misunderstood me."

"I hope so," said Miss Howard.

Hephzibah went on: "But the thing was a trifle, and a soul may have been saved from the world."

"From the world? nonsense!" cried Elizabeth, indignantly,—"for the Society of Friends. I was wrong to speak of your creed: it is good enough. But people interpret creeds oddly; and your friend who could have formed such an idea, and kept up such a low cheat, must have looked at the creed of Fox and Barclay as one looks at a noble landscape through a faulty window-glass."

"I did not mean to do thee a hurt," said Hephzibah, quietly. "Things appear differently to different people. I never supposed the matter could have seemed so monstrous to thee."

"Well," said Miss Howard, "I want you distinctly to understand me: it is not a case in which I would like to be misunderstood. What amazes me most about it is that you should ever have had enough doubt on the matter to make it worth while to talk to me about it."

"I did," said Hephzibah, firmly, "but it is as well to drop it now. Where is Margaret?"

"Marguerite is in the garden," said Miss Howard, coldly. "I will call her."

"Before thou goest," said Hephzibah, "I would say that I think no worse of myself to have asked thee a question."

"It seems to me, Hephzibah," returned Miss Howard, "that we are about to go over the same ground again."

"Well, I have in no wise changed my opinion," continued the Quakeress, "and, as thou knowest, I am not wont to change."

"No," said Miss Howard, smoothing her dress,— "no; but why you should not now and then, for variety, I do not see."

"Because," said Hephzibah, sitting very erect in her chair, and speaking with so expressionless a visage that it became a wonderful thing how the mouth had lost acquaintance with the other features and ceased to receive their assistance,—"because I am always right."

Miss Howard broke into the most merry of smiles. Her face was as wonderful in its power of change as was Hephzibah's in its frozen stillness. "Oh, Hephzibah, what a delightful woman you are!" she said. "I shall think of you all day for this." And over her mobile face flew gleams as it were of sarcastic expression and little storms of mirthful, half-controlled laughter. Then she paused a moment as she crossed the room, and turning said, "But if you are always right, Hephzibah Guinness, why not decide the question yourself for your friend? A Quaker pope who is infallible should not ask help of the ungodly."

Hephzibah said, quietly, "With help of the Spirit we cannot err, but I am not always sure. I do not think we should be always sure that we have spiritual guiding. I meant that we are right when we try to be right. There is the right of holiness and men's right. But I should have known that it was not well to carry my burden to one whose feet go along ways of ease and luxury, and have never had to choose which of two thorny ways to tread."

Hephzibah looked up as she spoke, and was shocked at the ghastliness of the face before her, which but a moment ago was alive with mirth. But the soul of a queen lay behind it, and a stern effort of will put down the unusual revolt in the woman's features. The doubts which arose in the heart of the Quakeress and broke into speech had power to call up for the other woman thoughts, remembrances, and difficult decisions which rushed upon her at once like an army of remembered evils, but were mastered again of a sudden, almost before Hephzibah had time to wonder.

Miss Howard wished to say nothing or to put the thing aside, but even for her strong will Nature was too powerful, and leaning across a chair-back, which she clutched with both hands, she said, "The past is its own. Bury it, bury it, Hephzibah Guinness, and as you value your chance to enter this house, never, never again speak to me of what I may have felt or done or suffered. It is a liberty, madam,—a liberty which I allow to no one."

"But thou knowest——" broke in Hephzibah.

"Enough!" returned Miss Howard, relieved and steadied by her passion of words, as emotion is always relieved by its outward expression. "Let us say no more of it. I have made a fool of myself, I dare say, and you must only remember what I meant, and not how I said it. For that I am sorry, because —well, because this is my own house. I will call Marguerite," but as she turned the girl she sought came dancing into the room, and at first, not seeing Hephzibah, who was hidden by her aunt's form, caught up her gown and with infinite demureness and grace made a low, sweeping courtesy, exclaiming, "You see I have not forgotten it, Aunt Bess? Isn't that the way they do it in the minuet? So,—not too fast—— Oh!" And she caught sight of Hephzibah, whom she both disliked and feared, and at once became erect and quiet.

The Quakeress looked at her sternly, while Miss Howard, passing the girl, said, "I leave you with Marguerite, Hephzibah: I shall come back in a few minutes."

As she went by her niece the girl plucked at her

dress furtively, and said in a whisper, "Thee will not go, Aunt Bess?"

"Chut, child!" murmured her aunt, bending down to kiss her, "she will not eat you; and if she did, you would surely disagree with her."

As Miss Howard left the room she reflected, "If I stay I shall only quarrel again with that woman. Better to go. Poor Marguerite!"

Meanwhile, the child stood in front of Hephzibah, a figure of guilty terror: children in those days stood before their elders until invited to sit down. Hephzibah was somewhat near-sighted, and this Marguerite knew. "Wouldst thou kindly excuse me a moment?" she said: "I will soon be back again."

"Come here," replied Hephzibah, curtly, "and sit down."

Marguerite was holding behind her, in vain hope to hide it, a long skirt of gorgeous brocade which she had borrowed from her aunt's wardrobe for her little bit of masquerade. As she sat down Hephzibah caught sight of the unlucky gown. "And shall this child, after all, go from us?" she said. Then, turning to the culprit, she went on, not unkindly: "A concern hath been borne in upon my mind, child, that thou shouldst be preserved in the meek life of truth. There are those who esteem lightly our testimony to plainness in attire. What is this that I see?" And she took up the edge of the broidered dress. "Why dost thou so offend against the discipline?"

Marguerite had much of her aunt's force of character, and by this time had recovered her composure. "Is it wicked?" she said.

"It will lead thee to no steadfast haven," said Hephzibah, "and the judgments of youth are vain judgments."

"But is it wicked?" she persisted, with set lips.

"It is not for thee to question the example of thy elders."

"Then Aunt Bess is wicked," said Marguerite, sturdily.

"She is hedged about with the snares of the world," said Hephzibah, sternly, "and hath counselled thee unwisely."

"I will not hear her so spoken of," answered Marguerite, flushing half with anger, half in shame, at this her first open outbreak. "She is the best woman God ever made: I wish I were like her."

Hephzibah disregarded the answer: "Dost thou read the Word? What portion art thou now reading?"

"Revelations," said the girl, shyly.

"And what hast thou gathered of good from them?" returned Hephzibah.

The child's face lit up: "I was made to think——" and she paused, not having meant to speak out her thoughts.

"Nay, child," said Hephzibah, "say thy speech out: I may come to understand thee better."

"I—I thought what would Penn and Fox say when they saw the gold pavements and the crystal walls and the color and beauty of the Master's house?"

"Surely the Great Enemy hath tempted thee," said Hephzibah. "Go to thy room and seek to be more wisely guided. Nay, wait," she added : " thou shouldst be punished." And she detained her by the wicked skirt as two men in the plainest dress of Friends entered the room and looked with amazement at the child's attire and her filling eyes. " Friends, you are come in good season," said Hephzibah, addressing them.

At the time of which we speak there had arisen among Friends what were then termed " great searchings of heart" concerning the preservation of discipline in the matter of dress and furniture. Mirrors were taken down; brass clocks received a coat of drab paint; in one case two aged Friends, on paying a visit to a rather lax member of the Society, were shocked to find on her floor the rare luxury of a dark carpet with red spots, over which they stepped, lifting their gowns and picking their way in grim reprobation. This is said to have so much annoyed their hostess that when they left she bore her testimony by carefully inking out all the offending spots of red.

The two Friends whose entry we have noted were overseers appointed by Meeting to examine into and correct breaches of discipline, and, regarding Marguerite as in a specially dangerous state, had called to remonstrate with her aunt concerning some points as to which rumor had reached them. Although living with her aunt, she was known to be really the ward of Arthur and Hephzibah Guinness, and to be in all spiritual matters within their control.

As they entered, Miss Howard, returning, met them with her stateliest courtesy. " I received a letter to-day," she said, "about my niece: what is there we can do to aid you?"

"They are come in good time," said Hephzibah, pointing to the poor girl's dress.

"Oh, my poor little woman!" returned Elizabeth, taking the child by the waist and holding her close to her. "This was but a child's frolic. I beg no more be said of it."

"It is of no great moment," answered the older of the men, "but we shall bid her to consider that she transgress not in future as to plainness of dress, and also of demeanor."

Elizabeth Howard flushed a little, but made no answer. She never ceased to fear that the child whom she so tenderly loved would be taken from her, as would surely have been the case had Hephzibah been able to convince her brother that this was either wise or right.

"What further can I do?" said Miss Howard. "I shall endeavor hereafter to see that she walks more straitly in the way you desire her to go."

"It is all," said the elder of the two. "We thank thee, friend Elizabeth Howard, for thy courtesy and temperateness, and will be going."

But Hephzibah felt moved to speak, and said, hastily, "As the child's guardian I would think it well that you asked leave of her aunt to see that her chamber conform somewhat more than it now doth to the plainness of Friends' dwellings. Because she is permitted to live with Elizabeth Howard, there is the more reason to ask that the child depart not from the teaching and simplicity of Friends."

"I do not permit strangers to wander through my house," said Miss Howard. "This has gone far enough. My temper is not unnaturally good, and I beg that it be not tried beyond what it may bear."

"What is this?" said Arthur Guinness, coming at this moment into the parlor, his good-humored, handsome face lifted by his tall form above the group.

"A star-chamber inquiry," said Miss Howard, with some heat.

Now the guardian had been much tried of late by the over-zealous, who thought him derelict in leaving his ward with her worldly aunt, and he wished to appease all concerned and to keep the peace.

The elder overseer explained the case, to the internal amusement of Arthur, who said, after a pause, "I agree with Miss Howard, but possibly she will oblige me by allowing thee to see the room where Marguerite hath her lessons."

Arthur Guinness had much weight with Miss Howard, and his mixture of grave sweetness and strong sense of duty, coupled with a keen and ready humor, all appealed to her pleasantly. "Well, yes," she said: "that is really the child's home in this house, as far as she has one apart, for she sleeps in my own chamber. Come, and you shall see for yourselves, and what you do not like shall be amended."

Upon this she turned, and, followed by the overseers, Hephzibah, and Arthur, led them up-stairs into a little sitting-room. It was so plainly furnished with books and a simple table and chairs that she felt herself triumphantly secure. Unluckily, between the windows hung a large round convex mirror surmounted by a gilded eagle and adorned after the French fashion with chains and elaborate projecting scroll-work. The two overseers paused before it.

"Thou wouldst do well, friend Arthur, to remove this vain temptation," said the younger.

"Friend Howard will no doubt thus oblige us," said Arthur, with a gleam of amusement in his face.

"But," said Miss Howard, "it is the child's. It belonged to her father, and I gave it to her."

"If it be thus," answered the older Friend, "it were seemly that we dealt with it as many Friends have of late submitted to have done with superfluous ornament."

"As you will," said Miss Howard, while Marguerite watched the group in profound curiosity.

Upon this the Friend produced from under the flap of his strait coat a long saw, and advanced upon the unfortunate mirror.

"What will he do?" said the child, alarmed for her small property.

"We shall but remove some of these needless ornaments," he said.

Elizabeth smiled. "Will you pardon me?" she said, taking the saw from his hand. "I am converted to your ways of thinking, and it seems to me that the handle of this useful tool has also a needless curving of vain scroll-work which cannot add to its usefulness. I shall be back in a moment." And so saying she walked out of the room, leaving the Friends to make what comments they pleased. In a few moments she came back, saying, "Thou seest I have, with the help of my man John and his woodsaw, despoiled the tool of its vain ornaments." In fact, she had had the handle sawn off.

Arthur Guinness looked at the useless tool and the blank faces of the overseers and the austere visage of his sister.

"It is not of much use, friend Elizabeth, in its present state. It seems to me," added the overseer, "we have in this matter been trifled with. The child should, we think, be removed."

Miss Howard broke in. "Enough of this!" she said. "I told you my temper was short. You touch nothing in my house, come what may. I have done my best, with better help from One I name not lightly, to keep this child in wise and wholesome ways. I will be ruled by you no longer. As to these trifles, which I think valueless or worse——"

"Then we had as well go," said Hephzibah.

"You have spoken the first words of wisdom I have heard to-day," said her hostess. And so with few words all excepting Guinness departed, apparently, save Hephzibah, without the least show of feeling or ill temper.

As they left the street-door the older man said, quietly, "Thou wilt do well to reflect;" and this was all.

"I have reflected," said Miss Howard. "Good-morning."

CHAPTER IV.

ARTHUR GUINNESS awaited Miss Howard's return in the parlor, walking to and fro under the half-dozen portraits by Copley and Stuart, and in and out, as a meditative man might do, among the nests of Chinese tea-poys, the carved chairs, and India cabinets. The walls were covered with small crimson squares of wall-paper, then just introduced, and the Quaker's foot fell noiselessly on the rich brown and yellow and red of a Turkey carpet. Arthur looked about him at the gay bits of china, and the masses of sombre color relieved by the brasses of the fire-dogs and fender and the flickering glow of the hickory backlog. Somehow it came to him, as it had done before, that it was pleasant, and that something in its well-attuned harmony made him comfortable and soothed him after the irritations through which he had just passed. He was of a speculative turn of mind, and was reflecting what a colorless world would be like, and how it would influence men. Then he paused to wonder what had become of Elizabeth, little dreaming that for the past five minutes she had been standing in the entry with her hand on the door, hesitating as she rarely hesitated. At last she steadied herself, and entered the room. Her decision once made, her natural sense of the humor of the scene she had gone through returned with full force, and as she came forward and shook hands with Arthur

Guinness she was laughing with the keenest relish of the elders' defeat.

"That was a rout," she said.

"Some victories are worse than defeats," returned Guinness.

Miss Howard's face fell. "You will never give up to them?" she said. "You will never take her from me? Promise me you will not."

"Thou art safe as to that," he said; "but wherefore make my task somewhat harder than it need be? Thou knowest that I must sympathize with my own people. It would have been easy for thee to yield in a matter so small."

"I could not," she said; "and if I know that you must sympathize with the folly of such extremes, I know also that you do not go such lengths willingly; and it is enough for me to feel sure that you will not part the child from me."

"But reflect a moment," he said. "If perchance I were to die,—as might be,—where, then, wouldst thou be in this matter? My sister would not hesitate a moment."

Elizabeth looked kindly up at his stalwart strength and smiled. "If you died life would be little to me," she said.

"And yet," he went on, coloring with pleasure, "thou wouldst still have duties, and most of all to this child."

"I do not think I should care then for anything. No, I do not mean that: you know what I mean."

"Yes," he said. "I do, and I do not. When years ago thou camest here from Carolina to meet the orphan of thy only brother, sent from France to join thee, thou foundest me and my sister, whom he had formerly known here, left guardians of the little one under thy brother's will. He, like myself, was a Friend: thou hadst left us to take the creed of thy mother. But I need not remind thee of all this afresh."

"No. It is still a wonder to me," she said. "It has been one long struggle to do right in the face of endless embarrassments. I may have failed——"

"Thou hast never failed to do what seemed to thee right," he returned, "and wilt not ever fail. But through all these long years I have loved thee as men rarely love. Nay, thou wilt not hinder me: let me speak. I love thee still. Time went on, and I came to know that while thou didst also love me——"

"I never said so," she cried.

"But thou dost, thou dost, Elizabeth! Thou wilt not say it, but thou wilt not say it is not so."

She was silent, and the dark look of sombre sadness grew, as it often did, upon her face, so that it seemed strange that such a face could ever smile.

"Thou art silent," he said. "Year after year I have asked thee to say what barrier stands between us."

"But you could not: you are a Friend. It is forbidden to you to choose where you will."

A great passion, half restrained for years, broke loose and took fierce possession of him. "I have taken wiser counsel than thine or mine," he said. "No man's will or wish should come between us. Speak, Elizabeth! Are they of Divine setting, the bounds thou wilt not break? Is it a sin to love me? Nay, that cannot be, for thou dost love me. Oh, my darling, speak to me! Who will more honestly counsel thee than I? who will more surely set himself aside to hear and help thee?"

Miss Howard dropped into a chair and burst into tears, covering her face with her hands, and shaken to the heart's core by the awful earnestness of the man and the terror of indecision which stole upon her lonely life.

"Wilt thou not speak?" he said.

"Nay, wait," she pleaded.

"I have waited long," he answered.

Then she lifted her head and saw the desolation of anxiety, of grief and pity in the brave face she had learned to love so well. "I cannot bear this," she went on. "I will speak though I die."

"But I cannot so hurt thee," he returned.

"No, I must speak now, for now as well as any day it may be told. Listen, and listen well, for never again shall I speak to you of this. It is my life I must tell you,—my life."

Then the two were still a moment while she resolutely regained the mastery over herself.

"I could tell you a long story," she said: "I will tell you a short one. I can tell it in one brief death-bed scene,—my father's. I shall never forget it. We were within hearing of the guns at the siege of Charleston, and my father was dying, and my mother away, and I was a lonely child; and I can see the room and the curtained bed, and the negroes about the door, and I only near,—I only of all who loved him. Then I recall the old black nurse saying, 'Honey, de massa want you;' and I was pushed forward to the bed. And I remember the curtained gloom, and the thin and wasted face within. And then I remember this, my father saying, 'Step back, aunty,'—you know how we call old negresses aunty,—'I want to talk to the child, and my time grows short.'

"After this I saw his great gray eyes looking suspiciously about until he made sure no one was near to hear; and when he was sure he said, 'Save thy brother, my child, there is no one but thee alive of all my race; and if I could see thy mother now, I would spare thee this, but I cannot. Therefore, thou who art a child must be as a grown woman, and remember what I tell thee, and speak of it to none unless thou must. I want thee to promise me that thou wilt never marry, because, my child, thou comest of an unhappy race. But when thou art older thou wilt look in a book which is in my desk, and which thy mother will give thee, and then thou wilt see what I mean, and thou wilt know why I say all this. And now I may not speak to thee longer; and I want thee to say only this, that thou wilt look in the book, and if I seem to thee to be right and just, thou wilt do as I say.' Then he spoke no more for a moment, until at last he said, 'Kiss me;' and after this my old black nurse lifted me up on to the high bed, and I kissed him and wondered why his breath was cold and why he did not take me in his arms; and then, although I cried, they took me away. This is all. And—— will you wait a moment?"

Saying this, she rose and walked steadily out of the room, while Arthur Guinness sat with arms crossed on his breast, awaiting her return. In a few moments she came back, and with a face like that of a judge delivering sentence of death she came towards Arthur, who rose to meet her, and said, " My friend, this is it: read it, and you will think with me. Read it, and you will never more ask me to marry. And now that it is done, how much easier it seems than I thought it! Perhaps, Arthur, because the burden is shifted on to other shoulders."

Arthur smiled: "When dost thou want this book again? May I look at it now?"

"No, no, not now," she replied, shuddering. "You must read it away from here. I—I—do not want to see your face when you read it."

"Well, well, Elizabeth," he said, cheerily, "I shall do as thou sayest; but it must be bad, indeed, to be as awful as thou seemest to think it."

"It is awful," she answered. "When you have done with it, leave it here for me if I am out,—in the drawer of this table. Good-by, Arthur."

"Farewell, Elizabeth."

As he left the house, Arthur Guinness looked curiously a moment at the faded little memorandum-book tied about with ribbon, and putting it in his breast-pocket went away down Front Street to his own home. Seeking his study in the back building, he laid the book on his table, and leisurely filling and lighting a pipe, let the bowl rest on his knee and thought a moment. He was more shaken and troubled than he cared to admit, even to himself, and was calmly waiting until he should feel himself once more fully master of his own emotions. Then he opened the book, and this was what he found:

"MY DEAR AND ONLY DAUGHTER, ELIZABETH,— Save thy brother, thou art the last of a race which has known so much more of sorrow than of joy that I beg of thee solemnly to consider what I have here written, that if it seem good to thee thou mayest come to see the matter as I see it, and to fulfil my wish, so that by never marrying our family misery may fall upon no others, and may end with us. HENRY HOWARD.

"MARCH 10, 1777."

Then came a number of entries:

"Richard Howard, Bart., of the Larches, Denbighshire, died Sept. 3, 1699, by his own hand.

"Of his brothers, John and Nicholas likewise thus perished.

"Margaret Wortley, æt. 30, daughter of Rd. Howard, Bart., died insane.

"The grandsons of Rd. Howard, Bart., were thy uncles; and of them none are left, they dying mostly of self-murder in like manner, but happily in foreign parts, so that the way of it is not known at home.

"And now are left only thou and thy brother, who, thinking on this matter with me, will die without issue.

"And so may we all find peace!"

Arthur Guinness let his pipe fall on the floor, and

turning to the table sat motionless, his chin on his hands, staring, as it were, with sad eyes into the future. He saw dim, changeful pictures of prosperous days to come, of a happy wife, of sons and daughters about his knees. Then he saw them grown up, and shuddering rose and walked to and fro in the room, until at last, feeling some fierce craving for larger movement, he took his hat and leaving the house strode hurriedly away towards the Schuylkill. To the day of his death he never forgot those hours of dumb agony. But long before night fell the strong habits of duty and faithful allegiance to common sense had brought him to the same decision which had guided and darkened the life of Elizabeth.

His walk took him along the willowy margin of the river, and at last across the floating bridge at Gray's Ferry, and so up to the high ground which lay back of Woodlands. At first there was in all his heart a sea of tameless passion, pent up for years, and only set free a moment, to be ordered at the next into quiet by a voice to him as potent as that which stilled the raging waters of Galilee. Then came for a while, or at intervals, that strange sense of being morally numbed which is like the loss of feeling mercifully bestowed on the physical system by the blow of the lion's paw. At last, out of the confusion order began to come, and painful capacity to study in detail his own sensations, and to look, though but unsteadily, at the need for decision. Then also he began to take note of outside things, and to see with curious intensity natural objects, from memories of which would come forth in afterdays all the large horror of the sorrow to which they had become linked by Nature's mysterious bonds of association. Thus he noted, whether he would or not, the miserly little squirrels, and the rustling autumn woods thick with leafy funerals, through which the lated robin flew in haste.

But, as I have said, at length, when he got back his power to reason and to be guided by the laws of action which long habit had made strong, there stayed with him, above all, a sense of pity for Elizabeth so vast and intense that to feel it was simply pain, and yet pain which ennobled and made strong. He felt that were she herself willing he could not now marry her; and out of a strange sense of duty to children yet unborn, and never to live, came at last peace and calm decision. Then he felt that he must see Elizabeth at once, and let her know how just he held her judgment to be.

In his trouble the hours had fled, and it was in the late afternoon that he reached his home.

Hephzibah met him in the entry. "Where hast thou been?" she said, looking in alarm and amazement at his mud-stained shoes and pale face. "Thou hast forgotten thy dinner, and the French minister has been here with whom thou wast going to Elizabeth Howard's."

"No matter," he replied, passing her. "I do not wish for dinner: I am going out again when I have changed my shoes."

"Thou hast had some worry," said Hephzibah. "I do think it concerns that worldly woman."

"Peace!" he returned: "thou knowest not what thou sayest. Nay, ask me nothing. If I have a sorrow, it is for no human ear."

"Hast thou asked her in marriage?" persisted Hephzibah, with a deep sense of gladness, "and has she refused thee?"

"I said peace," he returned. "The matter concerns thee not; and speak no ill of her, as thou lovest me."

"If it be as I say, thou hast been wisely dealt with, Arthur Guinness," she replied. A sense of triumph rang out in her tones despite herself, for this marriage was of all things that which she feared the most.

But Arthur went away up-stairs as she spoke, saying bitterly, "Ah, Hephzibah, in the field of the Master thou hast gleaned only thistles, and thy tongue is as the tongue of Job's friends. Never again speak in this wise to me. I am hurt and sore: let me alone."

An hour later Arthur Guinness walked quietly into the parlor of Miss Howard and awaited her coming. Presently she came into the room smiling, and took him by both hands, and said, "Sit down. I kept you waiting, as I was dressing, because I am going to a party to-night. And how thou must disapprove of my splendor!" And she made him a sweeping courtesy, and settling the folds of her heavy silk dress, sat down by the fire.

He looked up in wonder at her pleasant face. "How canst thou smile?" he said.

"How can I?" she said. "Some people are good, and their goodness helps them over the rough places;

and some have common sense, and that gets them through: now, I am not very good, and not very sensible, but I must have had a fairy godmother called Mirth, and when things are blackest I am perversely moved to smile; and that does so iron out the wrinkles."

"Oh, my darling!" he said.

"Please don't, or I shall cry," exclaimed Elizabeth: "I am often near it when I smile. You men never know how close they are together, laughter and tears. There! let us talk sensibly."

"I have put thy book in the drawer," he said; "and it is all over, and thou art right,—utterly, entirely right,—and—and—I shall never trouble thee more. Farewell!"

"Good-by?" she exclaimed, looking at his quivering mouth. "Not at all. Stay a little, just a little. I knew you would agree with me,—you always do,—because, as Hephzibah wisely remarks of herself, I am always right. It won't hurt you to know that I feel how much of sweetness went out of life when I found that you loved me, and that I must never think to sit at your fireside as a wife. But it was a decision of years ago, and I made it and unmade it. Yes, I did, for I am weak when you are by. But at last we have both made it, and I thought I should want to die as I told you; but I do not,—not while you live, and not while,—now don't look so sad,—not while there is anything on earth as amusing as the overseers and Hephzibah."

"What a droll woman thou art, my Elizabeth!" he said.

"Only a natural woman," she replied. "Do you regret what we have done?"

"No," he said, firmly. "I do regret the thing, not the decision upon it. I have only to look at the other side to be able to smile a little with thee."

"Then it is over," she said, "and we will get what we can out of life, with good help, Arthur, and set aside the past. Shall it be so?"

"It shall be as thou hast said," he returned. "And what else is it, Elizabeth?" for she stood up before him flushed and handsome.

"Only once," she said, "I must tell you how I love and honor and reverence you,—how gladly I would have trusted my life to you. I must show you once, as only a woman can, how I love you." And leaning over him as he sat she kissed him.

Arthur buried his face in his hands. "I thank thee." And the woman, crimson to the hair, turned and fled from the room.

CHAPTER V.

On the next morning Miss Howard received a note from Arthur, in which he said in a few words that he was going away for a fortnight, thinking it well that he should not see her face for a time. He went on to explain that it was not unlikely, owing to some commercial affairs, that he should before long have to go to Europe; and he added that he had meant to bring the abbé to see her, as he seemed a proper person to give to her niece the French lessons she wished her to take, but that the gentleman would call upon her at once.

Late in the afternoon of the next day the Abbé de Vismes walked slowly down Front Street, saluting as he passed them three or four of the French nobles who had drifted into this quiet haven out of the storms of European warfare. The abbé, to whom all lands were alike, provided the wines were good and the fare agreeable, had begun to make himself characteristically at home in the tranquil old town. As he passed Walnut Street he lifted his hat to the Marquis de Talons, and the pair exchanged pinches of snuff and walked on together among the groups of homeward-bound artisans and merchants.

"I am giving lessons in the dance," said the marquis, "but the times grow better, and before long we shall drink our Bordeaux again at home. What is it that you do to put the bread in your mouth, abbé?"

"The trade which is best," said the abbé, "is to turn Quakre, but I am grown too old to change; and, moreover, they drink not the wine of Madeira, which I find to be comforting and not dear."

"Thou hast reason," said the marquis, "but thy trade?"

"Ah!" returned the abbé, "my trade! That reminds me, and the place is here. I go to teach a young demoiselle the tongue of France."

"And is she as lovely as are the rest?" returned the marquis.

"Ah! I know not," said the abbé, "but my nephew, who has but seen her, raves of her as the young will do; and, as I said, this is the place. *Au revoir*, marquis." And so saying he went into the little garden, and was presently chatting with Miss Howard.

The parlor, with its pretty feminine belongings and pictures and china and well-rubbed tables and chairs, took the abbé by surprise, and the stately woman who greeted him with a courtesy which took up half the room no less delighted him. "Ah!" he said, "madame, I am enchanted to be again in a room with pictures and color, and, you will pardon me, with a woman who would have done honor to our court."

"You flatter me," said Miss Howard, smiling. "You have taken a leaf out of the book of your gallant countryman, De Lauzun."

"But madame will consider that I have lived here only among the doves which are called Quakres."

"Such as Miss Hephzibah Guinness," returned Miss Howard. "Well! well! I can weigh your pretty speeches now. But you have not seen my niece."

"And when better than now?" he said; upon which the pupil was promptly summoned.

"This," said Elizabeth, "is my niece, Miss Howard. And this, Marguerite, is the gentleman, the Abbé de Vismes, who will do you the honor to teach you French."

"She does not yet speak that tongue?" he said.

"No," replied Miss Howard.

"Then I may say, madame, *comme elle est gracieuse, cette fille!*"

The girl laughed. "Ah, sir, though I do not know French," she said, "I think you said something pleasant of me. It was thee, Aunt Bess, who said that a woman would understand a man if he said pretty things of her in Hebrew."

"And to be *spirituelle* seems to be of the family," said the abbé. "But you said her name was Marguerite, I think."

"Yes," said Miss Howard, "her mother's name. Her mother was French."

"Ah! and of what family?" inquired the abbé.

"We never knew her," said Elizabeth, briefly: "she died in France. Shall our lessons begin to-morrow?"

And after more chat and many compliments it was so agreed, and the abbé went away, doubly happy that he had a pupil and that she was beautiful to look upon.

The cool October days came and went, and the colder November mornings stripped off the last mournful leaves, while the French émigrés settled down to their work,—the abbé to his lessons, which began to be sufficient, the young baron to his novel labor in the Quaker merchant's counting-house. By degrees the exiled youth grew to like the quiet town with its splendid breadth of river boundaries, and to find friends among the rich and refined families to whom his name, and still more his frank and easy manners, gave him ready access. But above all other pleasures were the morning and evening walks to and from his place of business, for these led him past the garden and the buttonwoods, and the only house which was not open to him. Daily he lingered there, sometimes catching a glimpse of the blooming face he had learned to like so well, and sometimes seeing only the place which had come to be so pleasant for him.

By degrees, Marguerite in turn began to notice the handsome stranger who lingered as he went by, and looked happy when he caught her eye as she glanced up from her autumn garden-work of trimming the rose-bushes and preparing her plants for the winter. On this young and guileless heart no strong impressions had yet been made, and perhaps the very means which her aunt so sedulously employed to keep her free from all companionship with the other sex had but prepared her to feel deeply the first homage which a man should lay at her feet.

At length one morning she looked up from her book and said, quietly, "Aunt Bess, why dost thou not ask the abbé to bring the poor young man who is his nephew to see us? I see him go by here almost every day, and I think he would like to come in. I would if I were he."

Miss Howard turned towards her with a startled look. "Why," said she, "do you concern yourself with the young man? I dare say he has friends enough."

"But, aunt, he looks as if he would be nice to talk to, and he must have seen many things I should like to hear. And besides, aunt, why do no young men come here, and only Mr. Guinness and Hephzibah and—and—old people?"

"You will know some day," said Elizabeth. "Other young women may have friends who are young men, but you cannot, and you must not ask me why until the day comes that I may tell you why. Now you must trust me that what I ask is wise and right. Go back to your book again, my dear."

"Yes, Aunt Bess," she replied; and the truant locks fell over the volume, but their owner's thoughts strayed afar and made little castles for her in the land of Spain, such as young hearts are wont to build.

The morning after was cold and clear, and, early afoot, Marguerite was busy at her last tasks in the little garden, sweeping the leaves into corners and trimming the box borders. Presently, as she stood by the fence and threw over some dead branches, she was aware of a blush that told of her consciousness of the close neighborhood of the young baron. In her confusion she threw over with the lapful of trimmed stems her garden scissors and one of her gloves.

The young man touched his hat smilingly, and gathering up the articles in question laid one hand on the fence and leapt lightly over into the garden. "Mademoiselle will pardon me," he said. "These are her scissors. And we cannot be quite altogether stranger the one to the other."

"Oh, but you should not come in," cried the girl, naïvely: "my aunt will not like it. And my glove, too, if you please."

"*Mon Dieu!*" said the baron. "When it is that we enter the land of faëry we go not away without a souvenir. Mademoiselle will two times pardon me." And so saying, with his pleasant face glowing with mischief and evident admiration, he bowed to her, and kissing the glove thrust it in his bosom, and again leaping the fence, lifted his hat and went calmly away down Front Street, leaving her amused, amazed, and a little frightened. Then with quick female instinct she glanced a moment at the windows and cast a furtive look after the lithe, handsome figure which had disturbed her maiden heart.

The incident was a great one in her quiet life, but she said nothing of it to her aunt. Why, she could hardly have told herself, for in all things she was as frank as one could have wished so young a thing to be. Then the days fled by anew until midwinter brought an event which was destined to disturb all concerned in this story.

According as he had said, Arthur Guinness found, not now to his dislike, that affairs of moment made it needful that he should go to Europe. The chance to sail at once offered itself while he was absent in New York, and there was not time to allow of the four days' journey to Philadelphia and back again, if he would not lose an opportunity which might not recur for a month. Not sorry to put a little time between himself and Elizabeth, he seized the opportunity, and went away without seeing her again. Then a letter came, and another, and after that he had found his way to the Continent, and Miss Howard heard no more.

CHAPTER VI.

Meanwhile, an open winter of frequent sunshine ended in February with a week of intensely cold, clear, vivid days. On the late afternoon of one of these Hephzibah Guinness stood in her front parlor ready, in drab cloak and woollen stockings drawn over her shoes, to face the out-door cold. As she passed out into the entry, the knocker of the street-door sounded, and she herself opening the door was aware of young De Vismes, his face in a pleasant glow with the keen frostiness of the winter air.

"There is," he said, "madame, a packet which arrives from France, and there are letters which I am to carry to you; and behold them. It makes evil weather to-day."

Hephzibah took the letters, a large bundle, but did not ask the young man to enter. She had an odd dislike to foreigners and a half-confessed belief that they could all speak English well enough if they chose. "I am about to go out," she said, "so that I may not ask thee in."

"I wish you a good-evening," he returned, and left her.

The Quakeress went back into the house and hastily tore open the envelope. There was a long package within addressed to her. This also she opened, and within it found a large roll of folded pages, yellow and stained as if written years before. On the back it was addressed to the Abbé Gaston de Vismes.

"At last!" she said, "at last! Why must I decide anew? What I did was best for her. Yes, it was best; and now it is all to be thought over again, as if once in a life were not enough!" Then she looked at the other letters. There was one, a heavy one, for Miss Howard. "That at least may wait," said Hephzibah. Lastly, she fell upon a letter to herself from her brother. This she eagerly opened, and read with a haste as eager. It ran in this wise:

"DEAR HEPHZIBAH,—After many perils and grave occasions by sea and land, I have prosperously ended the affairs for which I came to Europe. Some business of a brother-merchant hath led me to the town of Nantes, where it hath been my fortune to be brought into relations with an ancient dealer, who, on hearing my name, and learning whence I came, inquired of me concerning a child sent to Philadelphia years ago on the death of its father, one William

Howard. Thou wilt be amazed to know that the child is our ward, Marguerite, and that she was the daughter of a lady of the class of nobles called De Vismes, to whom William Howard was married; and, what is yet more strange, I am told that letters which William Howard confided to this merchant were sent over to my care by the packet which came after the one which fetched our ward. These may have come while I was gone to Carolina to bring Elizabeth, but they seem to have been lost, although I do remember me plainly of the coming in of the packet, which was the George Arnauld.

"I send thee here the original papers, of which those lost were only copies, and with them a long and curious statement, with which I fear thou wilt not be well pleased. Thou wilt find that William speaks especially of a letter of instruction and of his will, which latter we did receive, and that he desires that in place of the child being bred in the ways of our Society, as he was at first minded and wrote, she should be left wholly to the wardship of our good friend Elizabeth. I pray thee at once to read the strange story William relates, and also his final letter, and then to give them to Elizabeth.

"Thou wilt learn that the child is now rich in this world's goods. I shall linger but long enough to secure to her this ample estate, and to place it in safety, and shall then return with all the haste I may to our own land.

"Thy always loving brother,
"ARTHUR."

Hephzibah set her lips sternly, and turned without a word to the longer paper, which she read and re-read eagerly. It ran thus:

"GENEVA, May 10, 1794.

"TO MY BELOVED FRIEND, ARTHUR GUINNESS, Merchant,—Thou knowest that after the child Marguerite was sent to thee, I did also despatch to thee my will and a certain letter in which I desired Hephzibah and thee to be guardians of the little maid. I did also provide for her bringing up in the ways of our Society, and for her living with my sister Elizabeth. But having been afflicted since the child went away to thee with bitter and, it is to be feared, mortal illness, I am come to think that I shall do more wisely to leave her in ward of my sister, Elizabeth Howard, so to raise her as may seem best to her, she being, although not of our Society, a woman seriously minded, despite some light ways of speech and vain jesting.

"Having thus provided by a letter of which a copy hath been sent to thee, I have it still on my mind to relate to thee the story of the child's parentage. If it had pleased Providence that I should have lived to care for her, I believe I should still have let her be looked upon as my child; but as it now seems unlike that I shall live to go home, I esteem it best to inform thee fully as to the fact that she is in no manner of my blood.

"Thou knowest that while I dwelt in England I felt a concern as to them that were afflicted in France. On this account I crossed over into that unhappy country, and journeyed hither and thither bearing testimony. Twice I was cast into bonds, and twice in danger of my life; but because of my being an American and of our Society, I was each time set at ease, and now of late have been left to do as I am guided. At last I came in the Eleventh month, which they call Frimaire, to the city of Nantes, on the river Loire, where, having a letter to one Pierre Porlat, some time a preacher of the Society of Protestants, he did kindly receive me into his house. A great gloom was come on all because of the cruelty of one Carrier, who hath put many to sudden death by drowning without even a form of trial.

"We comforted each the other with cheerful talk, and at last he confided to me that he had concealed in a vacant house next to his a young woman, a widow, and her little child, the husband, a Marquis la Roche, having been lately put to death. I was able to help these poor people by carrying to them food, especially at night, when we would sit in the darkness, a light being imprudent, and talk of many things, and of some good for speech and reflection to such as are in trouble. The young woman was of great beauty of person, and also of a singular calm sweetness, such as greatly moved my pity.

"At last on the evening of the fifteenth day of the Eleventh month, I came in from comforting some of the many who were in despair, and found Pierre Porlat and the woman La Roche set about by a guard of fierce-looking men. The poor thing had her little frightened child in her arms. I turned and followed them towards the prison. When we came near to the place, which is a low building called the Entrepôt, close to the water, we met eighty or more men and women tied in pairs and being driven like poor sheep—only these knew their fate—on to a boat to be sunk in the river. When they were counted the man Carrier said two were missing, and seeing the woman La Roche and Pierre, he said, 'Let these be added to make the count correct,' and threatening them with his sword, pushed them towards the river. Then the poor mother in her agony cried to me to take the child, and I went near her to do so, much moved, as thou mayst suppose. Then the man Carrier said, 'Who is this?' and one of the captains, named Lamberty, answered that I was a Quakre, as they say, and an American, and therefore a foe to aristocrats; upon which the man Carrier laughed and said, 'What carest thou for the citoyenne? Is she thy mistress?' Then I was filled with shame for her, and with great pity, so that I scarce could speak, and —may I be forgiven!—I replied, 'The woman is my wife.' Then they all laughed and said, 'Let the Quakre have his wife, and make haste;' and on this the woman and her child were set free. But they bade us stay and see the poor creatures drowned which were left. My friend Pierre cried out, 'The good God guide thee!' And after this I thrust the woman behind me, that she might not see this misery, and so stood in prayer while this great cruelty was suffered. Then I took her arm, and, carrying the child, went away into the town, fearfully searching my heart to see if the thing I had done was well.

"I lay awake all that night, and the next day I said to Édulienne,—which was her name,—'I have saved thy life with a lie, and thou art yet in peril. What I have done sorely troubles me.' Then she answered sweetly that I was a true gentleman, and that she would not be so saved, but would go and give herself up. But I answered that what I did I was moved to do, and that now the only true thing to do, both to salve my own conscience and to save her life, was to make her really my wife. On this she burst into tears, and could talk no more, but next day came to me and said it should be as I wished. And so, not to weary thee, we were married secretly by a brother of poor Porlat in the presence of his wife and daughter, all in tears.

"But my little woman scarce spoke afterwards, and pined away and died before spring, like one stricken,—perhaps of remembering her marquis; and, after all, I know not yet if that I did were well. But coming to Bordeaux, I found a master of a ship I knew, and gave him charge to carry the little one to thee; and this was in Fifth month of the year 1794.

"This paper will be left in charge of Eugène Perrière, of Nantes, merchant, who will see that it reaches thee in case of my death, with a copy of my instructions to my sister as to the governing of the child's life.

"Thy true friend,
"William Howard."

When Hephzibah had finished she rose, and folding the papers, went up-stairs to her brother's room and laid them in his desk, which she shut. "Let them rest there," she said, "while I think it over. Elizabeth may wait: there is no haste. They seem to have been long on the way, and he may follow them soon. There seems nothing but to give over the child to the world; and I can see the face of that proud woman when she hears it. Must all my years of anxiousness go for nothing?"

After this she walked to and fro in the room, as her brother had done when a blow as great, but far different, had fallen upon him. Years before, in a moment of too exalted trust in the wisdom of her own views as to how another's life should be ordered, she had destroyed the letter in which William Howard had wisely stated his altered opinions as to the education and religious training of the girl they had all believed to be his own. There are in every Church those who, if they held the reins of authority, would use them to force into their own ways of thinking all who chance to differ from them in belief; and of this peculiar mould was Hephzibah Guinness. Now the house she had builded with some fear and anxiety, but with no great doubt, was crumbling, and, as often happens, doubt began to grow as the probability of failure arose and increased; for it was plain enough to her that the one conscience she dreaded outside of her own—that of her brother—would be certain not to sympathize in the means by which she had secured, as she believed, the eternal safety of Marguerite. Night fell as she walked to and fro in the mazes of terror, doubt, and rudely-shaken convictions. At last, with a shock, came to her the idea that perhaps Arthur had written also directly to Elizabeth Howard; and at once, unable to bear the suspense through one night, she went down-stairs and out of the house. As she walked along the deserted streets, more and more clearly arose before her the spectre of Arthur's anger and reproach; but not for a moment was it plain to her that it would be righteous anger or just reproach. Yet it would be in some wise a falling off from her of the one thing in her life which was always sweet and fresh, and grew with a wholesome ripeness as years went on. Then, too, as she stood in the little garden, searching herself implacably to find if that which she had done was well, of a sudden the question took a new form, and pausing she asked herself if Arthur had himself done this thing, how it would have seemed to her sitting in judgment. Somehow, she could not carry out this idea. She stood in the night air, and tried to make for herself a picture, as it were, of Arthur burning the letter; but the figure she summoned up seemed to face her pale-visaged and grave, and would not act its part in the drama. With this a strange anger came over her, as if at the dear friend who was fated not to understand her; and then at last, with the despotism of a strong nature, she brought up her dominant instinct to put down these doubts, and saying aloud, "Thou knowest, Righteous Judge, if I have served Thee or not,—Thee, and Thee only," she knocked, and in a moment or two passed from her sombre thoughts into the life and gayety of Miss Howard's parlor.

The scene that presented itself to Hephzibah when she entered the parlor was not fitted to soothe or comfort her. At the table the abbé was showing

Miss Howard a new game of cards, which her niece was also learning unasked.

"No news of Mr. Guinness?" said Miss Howard.

"I have heard nothing," said Hephzibah, with a pang at the equivocation; and then reflecting that young De Vismes might have mentioned the letters, she added, "A package from him came to-day."

"Well, Aunt Bess," said Marguerite, "he must come home soon now."

Hephzibah was in a state of irritation which made any excuse for its display a good one. "Why dost thou call Elizabeth Howard, Aunt Bess?" she said. "The habit is unseemly."

The abbé looked surprised. He came of a world which took life easily.

"I like it," said Elizabeth, briefly: "it is my wish. Suppose we put aside our little questions of discipline till we are alone."

"All hours are good for a good purpose," returned Hephzibah. "Does the child learn also to use these tools of the Great Enemy?" she added, pointing to the cards.

Miss Howard's sense of humor broke out, as was her way. "Poor old Satan!" she said: "how much we put upon him! He might sue the whole world for slander."

"He has done so much worse in my France," sighed the abbé, "that we may pardon him these morsels of paper."

"The wrath of the Great Judge hath visited thy unhappy land," exclaimed Hephzibah, in measured and tranquil tones. "Evil hath come of evil,—

punishment of wrong-doing. He hath purged the threshing-floor: He——"

"Madame," said the abbé, some little remnant of nature stirring in him, "my mother died on the guillotine: you should of kindness fear to speak thus to one of my race. More than the wicked died,— women who were sweet and pure died; priests better than me; some who were young, and had not even lied ever in their lives. Ah, if we older ones were to die thus, we could without doubt find a reason to call it punishment."

Some remembrance arose and smote Hephzibah; but there must have been a cross of the Puritan in her breed, for these words came in answer: "Why He visiteth the sins of one generation on another is His alone to know; but we have none sinned so little that we may not accept punishment, and find a cause in us somewhere. Yet I did not mean to hurt thee."

The abbé rose and bowed silently, and there was a moment of awkward pause, when Marguerite said, "Oh, aunt, it must be time we went."

"Where?" said Hephzibah.

"We are going on to the ice to see the skating, and the coasting at High Street on the hill down to the river, and the bonfires, and——" And she paused, thinking what else or who else might be on the ice.

"Will you go with us, Hephzibah?" said Miss Howard, civilly but coldly. "I have promised Marguerite, as we shall be in the country far away from here next year, and perhaps she may never have another chance."

"You mean to leave us?" said Hephzibah. "Is not this a new plan? And Margaret? Is she to go? Dost thou think of taking her."

"Of course," said Elizabeth. "I go because of her."

"And my brother? doth he approve?"

"He does," said Elizabeth. "Any more questions, my dear?"

"No," replied Hephzibah, "but I thought thou wouldst——"

"Don't think for other people, Hephzibah: it makes half the mischief in the world."

"It is my duty," said Hephzibah, "to think for this child."

"Do not you think also," said Elizabeth, whispering in a quick aside, "that the abbé may come to believe we have more religion than manners?"

"That matters little," returned Hephzibah. "I will say no more to thee now. Farewell."

"Madame goes not on the ice?" said the abbé; and then, unable to resist, demurely added, "It would not make colder madame."

"I do not understand," said literal Hephzibah, "why it should not make me cold."

"I did say *colder*," said the abbé, while Elizabeth shook her fan at him, to his delight.

"I shall see you soon," said Hephzibah, and so left them.

CHAPTER VII.

It was a gay and merry scene on which the little party looked as they stood in their winter wraps at the top of the hill which sloped downward abruptly from Front Street to the river. The broad highway was covered with beaten snow, and at the river's brink a wide planking of wooden boards extended from the edge of the wharf down on to the solid ice of the stream. On either side bonfires were blazing, and lit with flashing glow the hipped roofs and red brick gables at the corners of Front and Water Streets. On the deep ice of the solid river, far over towards Windmill Island, fires were also seen, and around these swift-flitting figures on skates went to and fro, dimly seen for a moment and then lost in the darkness which lay upon all distant objects.

At the line of Front Street a crowd of the better class of people was gathered, intently watching the scene. Boys, men, and girls on long sleds were gliding every minute from the top of the hill. At first slowly, with noise and shouts of laughter, they started away: then the pace quickened and they flew past the fires on the hill-slope of the street, now seen, now lost, now seen again, until with a cry they gained the ice of the river and darted with delicious speed across the black, smooth plane of the silent Delaware.

It was the first time Marguerite had set foot on a

frozen river, and she had an odd sense of awe and insecurity. Then the wildness of the picture began to tell upon her quick and sensitive nature, to the abbé's amusement and pleasure, for he had become strangely fond of the charming little Quaker lady.

Here and there on the ice were bonfires, from which in every direction fell broad flaring shafts of rosy light broken by the long shadows of the skaters as they flew around the blaze. Many of the coasters also carried pine-knot torches, and as they dashed by the little party with cry and laugh the lights flared, and then sped away over the ice until they became but as red stars in the distance.

At last the girl urged that they should go over to Windmill Island, where hundreds of people were seen by the light of a vast fire engaged in barbecuing an ox. Here they lingered a while, and then the abbé, having learned that the ice was firm and safe, proposed that they should venture over a little towards the Jersey shore. Accordingly, they crossed the narrow islet, and walked some two hundred yards out on the farther ice. Here were no fires, but a dark quiet, with but a few score skaters who preferred the tranquil loneliness of the broader channel.

"How solemn it is, aunt!" said the girl as the black night grew about them over the dark ice, while, noticed only by Marguerite, a swift form on skates flew around them, now near, now far, in graceful curves.

Lured by the beauty of the faint moonlight on the ice and by the charm of the less-occupied parts of the frozen stream, they had gone some distance farther, when the abbé said abruptly, "What is that?"

A loud cracking sound came from the ice some distance below them. In this direction the river was partly open, and the gleam of the moonlight was visible on the clear water among the cakes of floating ice. As they stood to listen ten or twelve skaters clustered about them. Then there was another and a louder sound.

"The ice must be breaking up with the ebb tide," said Miss Howard, startled. "Come, let us get back to the island."

"Ah, yes, we shall do well to make haste," said the abbé, as the sounds, great and small, came quick and sharp through the keen, clear, frosty stillness.

At this moment the group scattered as if a bombshell had fallen among them. The skaters flew to right and left as a loud noise like a pistol-shot rang almost beneath their feet, while a crack ran along the ice, dimly seen as the cleft suddenly widened. The abbé and Miss Howard sprang back, and the latter, looking wildly around, cried out, "Marguerite! where are you? Marguerite!"

The girl in her curiosity at these mysterious sounds had ventured away a score of yards farther towards the open water. "Here, here, Aunt Bess!" she answered, running towards her aunt.

"Oh, my God!" cried Miss Howard. "My child! my child!" for the ebbing tide had broadened the cleft swiftly, so that as they stayed by the edge it had grown in a few moments to a space some five or six feet broad.

"Jump! jump over!" screamed Elizabeth. "We will catch you."

At this moment several persons came forward, and a tall young man on skates cried out in a voice of command, "For the love of the saints, do not move! It is now too late. Wait!" In an instant he was away, flitting back into the darkness. Then, when a hundred feet off, he turned short, and crying aloud, "Gare! gare!—I would say, 'Take care!'—place! place!" he skated with desperate energy straight towards the group, and, hardly pausing, gathered himself up at the edge of the rift and with a leap bounded over the open space of water, and coming down on the far side rocked to and fro, recovered his balance, flew along with the wild impulse of his leap, and returning in one long curve was at the side of the frightened girl. The ice was fast floating away.

"It is I," he cried. "I will answer for her with my life. It is I, Henri de Vismes!"

"My nephew!" exclaimed the abbé. "Be tranquil: he will take care of her."

"What shall we do?" returned Miss Howard.

"Get ashore," cried young De Vismes, "before the ice breaks. Seek men, that they do bring us a boat."

"Oh, my darling!" wailed Elizabeth.

"Have no fear," exclaimed the young baron, now hardly seen; and the ice, as they exchanged quick, agitated words of cheer and comfort and alarm, still moved farther and farther away. They could now only hear the voices of Marguerite and De Vismes, who themselves were no longer visible.

"Come," said the abbé. "There is to us but the one thing to do." And in silent horror Elizabeth followed him quickly over the ice to the shore of the island.

Meanwhile, the fretting river worked its will, and with crush and cry and groan and shocks the broken floes separated from the main mass and floated off, now grinding together, now thrust apart. The ice-island on which the two young people stood was about half an acre in extent, and quite safe from being overwhelmed. The danger was chiefly, as the baron knew, from the intense winter cold, which happily was made less terrible by the absence of wind.

The moment he was secure on the ice De Vismes said to Marguerite, "Have not fear, little lady: you are safe. It is but to wait."

"I am not afraid," she answered, "but I am sorry for aunt. And I thank you so very much: I do not think many men could have done that, and"—with a pause—"I am sure many would not."

The young baron laughed gayly: "It was nothing to do, and I could not have left you alone. I should have gone through the water that I might come to you. Is it not droll that we should know one another thus? *Je me presente, mademoiselle.* I am the baron Henri de Vismes."

"And I," said his companion, "am Miss Marguerite Howard." And she courtesied, laughing at the strangeness of the scene.

Meanwhile, as they talked, the baron undid his skates, and then, noticing that the girl shuddered, he said, "It makes very cold here. If it were that we had a bonfire!" Then he took off his cloak. "Put this around you," he added.

Marguerite insisted that she was warm enough. "You will freeze," she exclaimed.

"I am happy," he said, "and they who are happy do not suffer."

"Why are you happy?" said Marguerite, shivering. "I am sure I am not."

"Because," he said, quietly, "I am with you."

She was silent, and, innocent as she was, some instinct restrained her tongue while the cloak was thrown around her and the clasp fastened by two strong hands, which shook as they touched her throat.

"Let us walk," he exclaimed. "It is safe that we keep moving."

In this manner two hours fled away. Marguerite, despite the cloak, was shaking with the growing cold of the night, and De Vismes was becoming chilled and anxious. She begged to sit down, but the young man urged her to motion, and, taking her hand and laughing, made her run to and fro on the ice.

At last she said, "I am strangely sleepy: let me rest."

"To rest is to die," said he, calmly; and again they moved about, both of them silent and filled with a dread of which they did not speak, while the ice floated down the river towards the Point House, and the lights and the bonfires grew dimmer and dimmer.

After a long silence Marguerite exclaimed, "I cannot walk now: my head swims, my feet must be frozen: I cannot feel them. Oh, I shall die!" And, so saying, she reeled, and but for the ready arms which caught her would have fallen on the ice. De Vismes laid her down, resting her head on his knee, and without a word stripped off his coat and waistcoat, and, glancing anxiously and sadly over the water, wrapped his clothes around her, put his cap under her head and began to rub her feet. Presently she revived a little under the influence of one of those strange waves of reanimation which surprise the watchers by death-beds when life is slowly failing. "Where am I?" she said. "Who are you?"

"I am Henri de Vismes," he answered. "We are on the ice alone. Pray God they do soon come to us, or we die of cold!"

"I remember now," she said. "You said we must walk: I cannot walk, but you are a man and are strong. Do you run on the ice, and perhaps you may live to tell Aunt Bess how I loved her. You see, I am quite warm: I have no pain now—no pain." And her voice failed.

De Vismes was kneeling beside her as she spoke. "I shall not ever leave you," he said, "but soon I may not be able to speak. Therefore think not I shall go." And he caught her close to him, and as her head lay on his shoulder he said, "I did not mean to tell you until I had said it to your aunt, but now it does not make matter: I love thee. Canst hear me say I love thee?" And he looked piteously down at the dimly-seen face beneath his, and then across the cruel waste of rocking ice-floes.

She murmured something.

"What dost say, Marguerite?" And he drew her closer.

"I thought—there would be some one—who would love me—some day," she muttered. "Aunt Bess thinks not. Ah, she did not know." Then she was silent, and spoke no words in answer to his broken wail of love and pity.

De Vismes sat still, feeling, as did Marguerite, the cold less and less, and growing confused in mind and more easy in body. He saw the dim outlines of the splendid sweep of the Jura Mountains, the turreted château, the warm summer sun on the walnut-groves. He dreamed of warmth as a man who starves dreams of banquets. Then he thought how many De Vismes had died in the saddle, at sea, by the axe, and that he, the only one left, was to perish of cold; and then of a sudden he rose up, staggering and still holding the girl, and cried aloud, "Torches! lights! Wake up, wake up, Marguerite! wake! Saved! saved!" and reeling fell with her, while cries rang across the moonlit river and swift feet hastened from a boat along the ice.

When the young baron awakened from the swoon which had almost been death he was lying in a chintz-curtained bed with high mahogany posts. As his head cleared he saw by the dim light Miss Howard seated near the fire. "Mademoiselle!" he exclaimed. "*Mon Dieu!* where am I?"

Miss Howard was at his side in a moment, and drew aside the curtains. "You are in my house," she said, kindly. "Ask no questions now. You have been ill, very ill."

f

"But," he said, "*je m'en souviens*. Ah, yes, the ice!" And he started up. "And Marguerite, mademoiselle?"

"She is well," said Miss Howard,—"doing well."

"Ah!" he murmured, and, still feeble, fell back again.

After this the days went by, and with them memory returned, and he made out, as it were bit by bit, the scene on the ice, and learned that Marguerite had recovered even more rapidly than he. Then his uncle came to see him, and he began to get about his room, and to feel that he should no longer tax this generous hospitality.

CHAPTER VIII.

MEANWHILE, in Elizabeth Howard's bosom was raging a storm of emotions which taxed to the uttermost her unusual powers of self-control. For years she had sedulously, almost ridiculously, guarded Marguerite from contact with the other sex. She had told Arthur that she meant in the spring to remove to the country, and there to isolate her niece until she could fully make clear to her why she must never think of marriage, and why her life and fate must be different from those of a woman whom destiny had left free to love. With her her race must end. And now a pitiless accident had rudely broken the guard she had set about her niece · for in his ravings De Vismes had only too clearly told the story of his passionate first love.

But perhaps he alone loved; and at last she saw that he too must be told their miserable history, and that Marguerite's young life must also be darkened by this sombre knowledge. Miss Howard was not a person to abandon a purpose to which duty and a clear intelligence had guided her, and once resolved she waited only until De Vismes was well enough to bear an appeal to his honor and manliness.

In pursuance of her views she so arranged it that when De Vismes and Marguerite first met after their illness it should be in her own presence. There was to be no chance for sudden love-passages arising out of natural gratitude; and she was half amused, half sad at the awkward greetings which passed between the two as she brought them together in her parlor. But love has eyes as well as lips, and rosy blazonry on cheeks that glow with too warm consciousness of unspoken thoughts.

Just, however, as the scene was growing awkward, Hephzibah appeared, and after many questions asked and answered,—for the Quaker spinster was of a curious cast of mind,—she turned with her usual abruptness upon De Vismes, saying, "Thou wilt be going to thy lodgings soon, I suppose?"

"Yes," said the young man, coloring: "I have been too long an intruder here."

"We owe you too much to think you anything but one of our own household," said Elizabeth, while Marguerite looked up coyly thankful.

"Yet it is time that I went away," said De Vismes,

"but there will be no time that I shall regret to have been here. It will be that I go to-morrow."

"Is there no news of Mr. Guinness?" said Elizabeth.

"None of late," replied Hephzibah; and so saying left them.

The evening sped away pleasantly with cards and mirth, and the abbé told his little stories of the French court. At last, Marguerite having gone to bed and the abbé departed, De Vismes rose and said to Miss Howard, "This will be my last good-night in your house. *Bon soir, mademoiselle.* I shall be grieved to leave you: I shall not ever forget."

"Yes," said Miss Howard, rising, "it will be your last good-night here;" and she paused. "Will you be seated a little while? I have something to say to you."

De Vismes looked suprised, but with ready politeness sat down again, saying, "Is it that I can serve you in any way?"

"Yes," said Elizabeth; "more than you guess, perhaps more than you will wish."

"Mademoiselle does not yet know me," said De Vismes.

Elizabeth went on abruptly: "You are young and joyous, and life seems gladsome to you despite many sorrows."

"Yes," he said; "I have of late come to think of it as most sweet."

"And therefore," said she, sadly, "I think it cruel, even if in the end it be kind, to speak as I must do. You love my niece."

"Ah, mademoiselle knows it! she has guessed it! How kind of her to save a young man the awkward task to speak, to say he loves!"

"No more," said Miss Howard. "I know it; and you would have died for her?"

"Died for her, if it might be, a thousand deaths," said he. "I——"

"And if so," broke in Elizabeth,—"if that be true, would you give her up and go away if I show you that to marry her would be wrong—wrong to her, wrong to yourself—to your race, to your blood, to your children's children?"

De Vismes grew pale: "What is it mademoiselle would say? If that she will come to love me, why is it we may not marry? There is no shameful thing possible."

Miss Howard rose: the task was too hard for her. The frank, anxious young face followed her as she went and came. At last she paused: "There is in her blood, in my blood, a taint: we are born to be insane, to take our own lives. We are of a doomed race. We may not love as others do. God has set a curse on us. We may not marry; we may not see our little ones grow up and bless us as other women do. They would come to curse us when they knew. They would ask, Why were we born to this misery? Ah, it is a terrible thing that you have come to love Marguerite! But you will pardon me my abruptness: I meant to make it gentle, but how can I?"

De Vismes looked and felt bewildered. The suddenness of the blow indeed overcame him. "I will think of what you have said to me, mademoiselle:

I cannot now gather myself to think of it. I—I—never yet did hear of such a thing: I must have time to reflect."

"Reflect!" said Elizabeth. "No, no; you must act, not reflect. You love her; that is a reason to act. You must go away, and come back no more. You must never see her again on earth. Then I shall know how to save her. Oh, for God's sake, do not make it more hard for me! If you will not help me, I must tell her. How can I tell her?"

"But if she loves me," cried he, in despair, "how am I to go,—to go and leave her,—to see her no more,—to let her think of me,—a French gentleman, a noble,—as of a man who would say when as if about to die, 'I love thee,' and then fly and make no sign?"

"But I will tell her when you are gone," said Elizabeth. "You shall lose nothing in my hands. Surely you can trust me. And then she does not love you: I am sure she cannot. It will be you only who will suffer, and I appeal to you as a gentleman to save her. I am sure she does not love you."

"That may be," he said, sorely shaken.

"You ought not to hesitate," said Miss Howard; "you ought to go. Do not stay until you win her young heart, only that inevitable parting may break it. Why wait? You seem as though you would yield if you believed what I say. Ah, trust me, she does not love you."

"If this be so, I will go," said De Vismes, white as a sheet. "I will go, because you are right; but if I thought she loved me, I would trust to the good God's mercy and stay."

"Oh, my heavens!" cried Elizabeth, in despair. "She does not love you."

As she spoke, Marguerite glided swiftly into the room, crying out, "You have no right to speak for me, Aunt Bess. I—I came down because I had forgotten to kiss you good-night, and I heard you. I—I—— Oh, Aunt Bess, I do love him! Is it wrong?"

"Marguerite!" said De Vismes; and he caught her in his arms.

"Oh, my children!" exclaimed Elizabeth. As she spoke the knocker sounded again and again.

"What is that?" said Miss Howard. "It is late; what can it be?" And the little commonplaces of life broke into their storm of fears and hopes and made a sudden quiet.

"I will go to see," said De Vismes, "if you please. The maid must have gone to bed. They knock again."

"Yes, oblige me by seeing who it is. They seem in haste," said Elizabeth.

De Vismes went into the entry and hastily opened the door. He fell back in amazement as Hephzibah, not recognizing him, went past him with no more notice than to say, "Is thy mistress in the parlor?" and then suddenly broke into the room.

Elizabeth and Marguerite rose in amazement.

Hephzibah stood still an instant in the doorway, her drab cloak dripping, her scant gray locks fallen about her face and neck, without bonnet or other headgear.

"What is it?" cried Miss Howard.

Hephzibah seized her arm and leaned forward. "He is dead!" she said. "Thou hast killed him."

"I? Who?" exclaimed Elizabeth.

"Arthur, my Arthur, my brother Arthur! Do not look at me so. Go down on thy knees and pray for forgiveness."

"For Heaven's love," said Elizabeth, "what is it, woman? Did you say Arthur was dead? Tell me about it. I—I never did trust you: this cannot be."

"He is dead," said Hephzibah,—"drowned,—the ship lost,—the news just come. I loved no one like him. Why didst thou deny him the poor gift that would have kept him here?"

"If," said Elizabeth, "my dear Arthur is gone to God, I am answerable to the dead alone. My love! my love!" And she sank into a chair in a passion of tears, while De Vismes and her niece ran to her side and silently stood by her as if to comfort and protect her.

Hephzibah, white, trembling, with hands knitted in front of her, and with working fingers, remained alone and speechless, looking down upon the little group. At last she said, with a curious unnatural firmness, "There are many things to talk of, Elizabeth Howard."

Elizabeth looked up. "Are you of flesh and blood, woman?" she cried. "Go! go away! I cannot talk with you to-night. Take her home, some one."

"That were best," said De Vismes.

"I should better do my Master's errand were I to

forget on His service the loved one I have lost," returned Hephzibah. "To-day is His time. To-morrow,—to-morrow—— Who owns to-morrow? Had I been more ready in the past to warn my brother of the snares of the worldlings, he might yet be alive."

"Go!" said Miss Howard. And De Vismes took the Quakeress kindly but firmly by the arm, saying, "Come; the time is not well for speech." And they turned and left the room.

"Poor Aunt Bess!" cried Marguerite. "If only I could do something for you!"

"Only One can do that, my child," said Elizabeth.

CHAPTER IX.

The news of Arthur Guinness's death fell with varied influence upon those who were near or dear to him.

An awful temptation was by Fate put away from the path of Miss Howard. The man she loved was taken, and with him went, as she knew only too well, much of the little sunshine of her life. It was more like widowhood to her than such a loss would have been to a younger woman; and it was characteristic of the woman and of her life that after the first sharp anguish she accepted her new sorrow as brave men accept sentence of death, and that with eyes more than ever set on the future she took up the threads of duty anew, and went sweetly and pleasantly along the ways of life.

To Hephzibah she was that enigma which a person with a strong overruling sense of humor must always be to one who knows no note in the wide gamut of mirth-making thoughts. That, as time went on, Miss Howard could smile,—nay, worse, laugh,—that the little events of daily life could still afford her amusement, seemed to Hephzibah a constant insult to her brother's memory. But some laugh through life,— laugh if they win or lose; and some cry if they always win; and Elizabeth would have gone with a smile to any fate which life could bring. The exasperation which this temperament wrought on Hephzibah had unhappily evil consequences, and perhaps was the overweight which turned the balance of her decisions.

Her brother's death left her possessed of the papers which would give her steady control over the spiritual destinies of Marguerite, whose sole guardian she now became. She found it easy to assure herself that a fortune was bad for the girl,—that to fall under Elizabeth's entire rule was yet more evil for the child. Then, too, Elizabeth, goaded to despair by her new assumptions as time went by, rose in revolt, as any noble nature must have done, until at last Hephzibah became more and more certain that nothing could be surer spiritual death for her ward than the fate which would be hers if the later wishes of William Howard became known. Come what might, a long while must elapse before it became clear through other sources that the child was not destined to Quakerism. Letters were lost every week in those days, and war everywhere made it as likely as not that years would pass before the truth was made manifest. Therefore it was that the letters lay in Arthur Guinness's desk safe enough, and that the months fled away and the spring came.

Meanwhile, Marguerite went listlessly about her daily tasks, with a sense that much of the sweetness of her young life had gone from her; for, after one or two more interviews with her lover, she had been told by Miss Howard the dark story of her race, and had come at last, like De Vismes and Arthur Guinness, to acquiesce in the decree by which Elizabeth had forbidden for them as for herself the thought of love or marriage.

It was the old, sad, beautiful tale of love controlled by duty. But to see one another, to meet and to part with no utterance of their forbidden love, was fast becoming a task too grave for youthful human hearts. The baron felt that it behooved him as a man to end the ever-renewed struggle by leaving the city. Therefore on an afternoon in the end of May there was a scene in Miss Howard's home of bitter final parting, from which De Vismes tore himself away with the sobs of Marguerite echoing in his ears. He went out through the paling fence, and moved westward along Shippen to Argyle Street, half consciously avoiding the ways where he could meet faces that he knew. Here he turned westward on his favorite walk towards the Neck, along Kingsessing Road, then lined with fields and pasture-grounds, and presently felt a kindly arm on his own and heard his uncle say, "Thou hast been hurt of a woman, my dear. Shall I be disagreeable to walk with thee? I know that fortune went not well with thee, Henri, because we are poor and friendless. Were it not so, thy Quaker maid had not said nay to one of our house."

"But, uncle," said the baron, "it is still as I told thee. There is more to put us one from the other than the want of love. It is not my secret, and I cannot tell thee."

"As thou pleasest," said the abbé. "Women are alike all the world over: men may vary, but women never. Ah, if I could but endow thee with my experience, thou mightst have good luck with the lady. And she is handsome too, and I am told will have a good dot. One acquires experience too late."

The baron was silent, as his mood fitted not with the abbé's cynical ways, and they walked along quietly. By and by they came upon the Penrose Ferry Road, and the frogs began to croak their vespers and a faint haze rose up over the broad meadows of the Neck lands, while the setting sun, large, round, and crimson, hung on the far horizon's verge across the Schuylkill. A windmill's sails turned slowly on the left of the road, and the sound of the milking-pans and the lowing of cows crossed the flat pastures and ditches, and came pleasantly to the ears of the exiles as they paused to listen, soothed by the peaceful sweetness of the hour. Then a flock of sheep came along the road, and as they jostled one another the dust of the highway made a cloud of rosy gold over and about them and the herdsman who walked behind in a check cloak and slouched hat.

"It is like our Normandy," said the abbé. "But, *mon Dieu*, what is this?" for as he spoke they were aware of a tall, largely-made man coming towards them with quick steps.

The baron darted forward: "It is—is it?—nay, it is you, Mr. Guinness! Where is it that you have come from? We have thought you dead."

"Ah, this is most happy," cried the abbé.

"By the will of Providence," said Arthur, "it is indeed I,—a man saved after shipwreck and many perils. I landed at New Castle to-day, and made haste to drive home, but, my carriage breaking down, I am come these last few miles afoot. Are all well,—Elizabeth, Hephzibah, Marguerite?"

"All," said the baron; "and what joy will there be!"

Then Arthur went on to tell his story, and at last it was agreed that the abbé should hasten in advance to tell Hephzibah, and that the baron should also warn Miss Howard, lest the women should be too much startled by this sudden return of Arthur.

The abbé reached Miss Guinness's house a half-hour after, and with what result we shall presently hear. When, still later, he entered Miss Howard's home, he found the little group, half in tears, half in laughter, surrounding the dear friend who had so unexpectedly come back. Elizabeth was saying to the baron, "It was good and thoughtful of you to come beforehand and tell me. I thank you." And then a small hand stole furtively into his, and he felt by its tender touch that he was still better thanked.

"But what ails thee, friend De Vismes?" said Arthur; and all turned to look at the abbé, who was flushed and excited.

"Oh, a thing most strange," replied the abbé, "and I must tell it."

"Why not?" said Miss Howard, looking up with flushed and joyful face.

"And I must leave thee," said Arthur. "It was on my way to pass here, and I could not go by without a word; but now I would seek Hephzibah."

"She is not in her house," said the abbé; "and before you go I may ask that a thing be for me made clear."

"And what?" said Arthur. "Tell us soon, for I may not tarry on my way home."

"I did go," said the abbé, "with haste to tell mademoiselle the sister of your soon coming, but the small maid gave me assurance that she was not at home; and then I did think I would leave a word written to say all I had to say; and that I might write I was asked of the maid to go into the room of M. Guinness, where sometimes we have smoked. And when, the maid having opened the desk and left me, I ended the little note, I saw with amazement on a bundle of papers which had a look to be old the name of me, Gaston de Vismes, abbé. And as it seemed of my address, I did not attend long before I unfolded the sheets and read. What I read was to me as a dream, as a dream of the past, as a tale of the dead,—of my sister. I am troubled: I say, 'This is mine.' I find in the leaves a letter of Miss Howard: I bring it too, I bring all. You will make for me excuses. This paper is what the dead say. It disturbs me, I am shaken. Here is the letter for you, Mademoiselle Howard."

At this moment Hephzibah entered the room; she had come by an accident hither. She saw first in the abbé's hands the papers she had concealed, and heard his last rapid, troubled sentences.

"Thou hast stolen my papers," she said, coldly; and then of a sudden, as she advanced a step, she caught sight of Arthur, who ran forward as she spoke.

"Hephzibah! sister!" he cried, "I am come again. Our heavenly Father has heard thy prayers."

"Arthur!" she said, and for a brief moment, locked in his strong arms, she remembered only that this one loved heart yet beat. But then suddenly there came upon her the horror and fear of the discovery which was about to spring upon her. She was not a woman to wait her fate or keep silence, hoping to escape. While the little group watched this solemn meeting of the brother and sister she gathered herself up, calmly adjusted her gray bonnet, and said, "Wilt thou come home with me, Arthur? I have much to say. These papers were in a cover addressed by thee to me: I will take them now." And she moved towards the amazed abbé.

"Nay," said Elizabeth, "it seems that they belong to the abbé. And my own letter, it has a distant date. Why, woman, did you really dare to keep this from me?"

"What does this mean?" said Arthur; and all eyes turned upon Hephzibah.

"Give me my papers," she said. "We should talk of them alone, Arthur."

"But," said the abbé, "I have read them."

"Thou hast read them?" said Hephzibah, in measured tones.

"Why not?" exclaimed Arthur, puzzled.

"And they say that it was my sister, the Marquise de la Roche, which Mr. Howard did marry to save from death; and the child is my niece, and not his daughter."

"Impossible!" said Elizabeth. "What dream is this?" And she seized the girl as if fearing to lose her, and added, "But you kept these papers, Hephzibah? You thought Arthur dead: you meant to keep them always. Oh, woman! woman! how could you? Arthur, I would not have told this: I did not know. I am sorry: I pity her."

"Thou hast no need," said Hephzibah. "What I did was under a concern, but the way has not opened, and I am freed."

"Oh, Hephzibah!" exclaimed Arthur, and sinking into a chair he covered his face.

"I am grieved only to have hurt thee, brother," said Hephzibah. "The girl is lost to Friends: the world hath her."

"And," cried the young De Vismes, "she is of our own blood,—my cousin! *Ah, mon âme!*" And he caught the bewildered girl in his arms, while Hephzibah turned quietly and went out into the street.

THEE AND YOU.

Once on a time I was leaning over a book of the costumes of forty years before, when a little lady said to me, "How ever could they have loved one another in such queer bonnets?" And now that since then long years have sped away, and the little critic is, alas! no longer young, haply her children, looking up at her picture, by Sully, in a turban and short waist, may have wondered to hear how, in such disguise, she too was fatal to many hearts, and set men by the ears, and was a toast at suppers in days when the waltz was coming in and the solemn grace of the minuet lingered in men's manners.

And so it is, that, calling up anew the soft September mornings of which I would draw a picture before they fade away with me also, from men's minds, it is the quaintness of dress which first comes back to me, and I find myself wondering that in nankeen breeches and swallow-tailed blue coats with buttons of brass once lived men who, despite gnarled-rimmed beavers and much wealth of many-folded cravats, loved and were loved as well and earnestly as we.

I had been brought up in the austere quiet of a small New England town, where life was sad and manners grave, and when about eighteen served for a while in the portion of our army then acting in the North. The life of adventure dissatisfied me with my too quiet home, and when the war ended, I was glad to accept the offer of an uncle in China to enter his business house. To prepare for this it was decided that I should spend six months with one of the great East India firms. For this purpose I came to Philadelphia, and by and by found myself a boarder in an up-town street, in a curious household ruled over by a lady of the better class of the people called Friends.

For many days I was a lonely man among the eight or ten persons who came down, one by one, at early hours to our breakfast-table and ate somewhat silently and went their several ways. Mostly, we were clerks in the India houses which founded so many Philadelphia fortunes, but there were also two or three of whom we knew little, and who went and came as they liked.

It was a quiet lodging-house, where, because of being on the outskirts and away from the fashion and stir of the better streets, those chiefly came who could pay but little, and among them some of the luckless ones who are always to be found in such groups,—stranded folks, who for the most part have lost hope in life. The quiet, pretty woman who kept the house was of an ancient Quaker stock which had come over long ago in a sombre Quaker May-flower, and had by and by gone to decay, as the best of families will. When I first saw her and some of her boarders it was on a pleasant afternoon early in September, and I recall even now the simple and quiet picture of the little back parlor where I sat down among them as a new guest. I had been tranquilly greeted, and had slipped away into a corner behind a table, whence I looked out with some curiosity on the room and on the dwellers with whom my lot was to be cast for a long while to come. I was a youth shy with the shyness of my age, but having had a share of rough, hardy life, ruddy of visage and full of that intense desire to know things and people that springs up quickly in those who have lived in country hamlets far from the stir and bustle of city life.

The room I looked upon was strange, the people strange. On the floor was India matting, cool and white. A panel of painted white woodwork ran around an octagonal chamber, into which stole silently the evening twilight through open windows and across a long brick-walled garden-space full of roses and Virginia creepers and odorless wisterias. Between the windows sat a silent, somewhat stately female, dressed in gray silk, with a plain muslin cap about the face, and with long and rather slim arms tightly clad in silk. Her fingers played at hide-and-seek among some marvellous stitchery,—evidently a woman whose age had fallen heir to the deft ways of her youth. Over her against the wall hung a portrait of a girl of twenty, somewhat sober in dress, with what we should call a Martha Washington cap. It was a pleasant face, unstirred by any touch of fate, with calm blue eyes awaiting the future.

The hostess saw, I fancied, my set gaze, and rising came toward me as if minded to put the new-comer at ease. "Thee does not know our friends?" she said. "Let me make thee known to them."

I rose quickly and said, "I shall be most glad."

We went over toward the dame between the windows. "Grandmother," she said, raising her voice, "this is our new friend, Henry Shelburne, from New England."

As she spoke I saw the old lady stir, and after a moment she said, "Has he a four-leaved clover?"

"That is what she always says. Thee will get used to it in time."

"We all do," said a voice at my elbow; and turning, I saw a man of about thirty years old, dressed in the plainest-cut Quaker clothes, but with the contradiction to every tenet of Fox written on his face, where a brow of gravity forever read the riot act to eyes that twinkled with ill-repressed mirth. When I came to know him well, and saw the preternatural calm of his too quiet lips, I used to imagine that unseen little demons of ready laughter were forever twitching at their corners.

"Grandmother is very old," said my hostess.

"Awfully old," said my male friend, whose name proved to be Richard Wholesome.

"Thee might think it sad to see one whose whole language has come to be just these words, but sometimes she will be glad and say, 'Has thee a four-leaved clover?' and sometimes she will be ready to cry, and will say only the same words. But if thee were to say, 'Have a cup of coffee?' she would but answer, 'Has thee a four-leaved clover?' Does it not seem strange to thee, and sad? We are used to it, as it might be,—quite used to it. And that above her is her picture as a girl."

"Saves her a deal of talking," said Mr. Wholesome, "and thinking. Any words would serve her as well. Might have said, 'Topsail halyards,' all the same."

"Richard!" said Mistress White. Mistress Priscilla White was her name.

"Perchance thee would pardon me," said Mr. Wholesome.

"I wonder," said a third voice in the window, "does the nice old dame know what color has the clover? and does she remember fields of clover,—pink among the green?"

"There is a story," said Priscilla, "that when my grandmother was yet a young woman, my grandfather on the day that he died,—his death being sudden,—fetched her from the field a four-leaved clover, and so the memory of it clings while little else is left."

"Has thee a four-leaved clover?" re-echoed the voice feebly from between the windows.

The man who was curious as to the dame's remembrances was a small stout person whose arms and legs did not seem to belong to him, and whose face was strangely gnarled, like the odd face a boy might carve on a hickory-nut, but was withal a visage pleasant and ruddy.

"That," said Mistress White as she moved away, "is Mr. Schmidt,—an old boarder with some odd ways of his own which we mostly forgive. A good man—if it were not for his pipe," she added demurely,—"altogether a good man."

"With or without his pipe," said Mr. Wholesome.

"Richard!" returned our hostess, with a half smile.

"Without his pipe," he added; and the unseen demons twitched at the corners of his mouth anew.

Altogether, these seemed to me droll people, they said so little, and, saving the small German, were so serenely grave. I suppose that first evening must have made a deep mark on my memory, for to this day I recall it with the clearness of a picture still before my eyes. Between the windows sat the old dame with hands quiet on her lap now that the twilight had grown deeper,—a silent, gray Quaker sphinx, with only one remembrance out of all her seventy years of life. In the open window sat as in a frame the daughter, a woman of some twenty-five years, rosy yet as only a Quakeress can be when rebel nature flaunts on the soft cheek the colors its owner may not wear on her gray dress. The outline was of a face clearly cut and noble as if copied from a Greek gem,—a face filled with a look of constant patience too great perhaps for one woman's share, with a certain weariness in it also, yet cheerful too, and even almost merry at times,—the face of one more thoughtful of others than of herself, and, despite toil and sordid cares, a gentlewoman, as was plain to see. The shaft of light from the window in which she sat broadened into the room, and faded to shadow in far corners among chairs with claw toes and shining mahogany tables,—the furniture of that day, with a certain flavor about it of elegance, reflecting the primness and solidness of the owners. I wonder if to-day our furniture represents us too in any wise? At least it will not through the generations to follow us: of that we may be sure. In the little garden, with red gravelled walks between rows of box, Mr. Schmidt walked to and fro, smoking his meerschaum,—a rare sight in those days, and almost enough to ensure your being known as odd. He walked about ten paces, and went and came on the same path, while on the wall above a large gray cat followed his motions to and fro, as if having some personal interest in his movements. Against an apricot tree leaned Mr. Wholesome, watching with gleams of amusement the cat and the man, and now and then filliping at the cat a bit of plaster which he pulled from the wall. Then she would start up alert, and the man's face would get to be quizzically unconscious; after which the cat would settle down and the game begin anew. By and by I was struck with the broad shoulders and easy way in which Wholesome carried his head, and the idea came to me that he had more strength than was needed by a member of the Society of Friends, or than could well have been acquired with no greater exercise of the limbs than is sanctioned by its usages. In the garden were also three elderly men, all of them quiet and clerkly, who sat on and about the steps of the other window and chatted of the India ships and cargoes, their talk having a flavor of the spices of Borneo and of well-sunned madeira. These were servants of the great India houses when commerce had its nobles, and lines were sharply drawn in social life.

I was early in bed, and rising betimes went down to breakfast, which was a brief meal, this being, as Mr. Wholesome said to me, the short end of the day. I should here explain that Mr. Wholesome was a junior partner in the house in which I was to learn the business before going to China. Thus he was the greatest person by far in our little household, although on this he did not presume, but seemed to me greatly moved toward jest and merriment, and to sway to and fro between gayety and sadness, or at the least gravity, but more toward the latter when Mistress White was near, she seeming always to be a checking conscience to his mirth.

On this morning, as often after, he desired me to walk with him to our place of business, of which I was most glad, as I felt shy and lonely. Walking down Arch Street, I was amazed at its cleanliness, and surprised at the many trees and the unfamiliar figures in Quaker dresses walking leisurely. But what seemed to me most curious of all were the plain square meeting-houses of the Friends, looking like the toy houses of children. I was more painfully impressed by the appearance of the graves, one so like another, without mark or number, or anything in the disposition of them to indicate the strength of those ties of kinship and affection which death had severed. Yet I grew to like this quiet highway, and when years after I was in Amsterdam the resemblance of its streets to those of the Friends here at home overcame me with a crowd of swift-rushing memories. As I walked down of a morning to my work, I often stopped as I crossed Fifth Street to admire the arch of lindens that barred the view to the westward, or to gaze at the inscription on the Apprentices' Library, still plain to see, telling that the building was erected in the eighth year of the Empire.

One morning Wholesome and I found open the iron grating of Christ Church graveyard, and passing through its wall of red and black glazed brick, he turned sharply to the right, and coming to a corner bade me look down where, under a gray plain slab of worn stone, rests the body of the greatest man, as I have ever thought, whom we have been able to claim as ours. Now a bit of the wall is gone, and through a railing the busy or idle or curious, as they go by, may look in and see the spot without entering.

Sometimes, too, we came home together, Wholesome and I, and then I found he liked to wander and zigzag, not going very far along a street, and showing fondness for lanes and byways. Often he would turn with me a moment into the gateway of the University Grammar School on Fourth Street, south of Arch, and had, I thought, great pleasure in seeing the rough play of the lads. Or often, as we came home at noon, he liked to turn into Paradise Alley, out of Market Street, and did this, indeed, so often that I came to wonder at it, and the more because in an open space between this alley and Commerce Street was the spot where almost every day the grammar-school boys settled their disputes in the way more common then than now. When first we chanced on one of these encounters, I was surprised to see Mr. Wholesome look about him as if to be sure that no one else was near, and then begin to watch the combat with a strange interest. Indeed, on one occasion he utterly astonished me by taking by the hand a small boy who had been worsted and leading him with us, as if he knew the lad, which may well have been. But presently he said, "Reuben thee said was thy name?" "Yes, sir," said the lad. "Well," said Mr. Wholesome,—after buying him a large and very brown horse gingerbread, two doughnuts, and a small pie,—"when you think it worth while to hit a fellow, never slap his face, because then he will strike you hard with his fist, which hurts, Reuben. Now, mind: next thee strikes first with the fist, my lad, and hard, too." If I had seen our good Bishop White playing at taws, I could not have been more overcome, and I dare say my face may have shown it, for, glancing at me, he said demurely, "Thee has seen in thy lifetime how hard it is to get rid of what thee liked in thy days of boyhood." After which he added no more in the way of explanation, but walked along with swift strides and a dark and troubled face, silent and thoughtful. I observed many times after this that the habits and manners of Friends sat uneasily on Mr. Wholesome, and that when excited he was quite sure to give up for a time his habitual use of Friends' language, and to let slip now and then phrases or words which were in common use among what Mistress Priscilla called world's people. It was a good while before I came to understand the source of these peculiar traits.

Sometimes in the early morning I walked to my place of business with Mr. Schmidt, who was a man so altogether unlike those about him that I found in him a new and varied interest. He was a German, and spoke English with a certain quaintness and with the purity of speech of one who has learned the tongue from books rather than from men. I found after a while that this guess of mine was a good one, and that, having been bred an artist, he had been put in prison for some political offence, and had in two years of loneliness learned English from our older authors. When at last he was set free he took his little property and came away with a bitter heart to our freer land, where, with what he had and with the lessons he gave in drawing, he was well able to live the life he liked in quiet ease and comfort. He was a kindly man in his ways, and in his talk gently cynical; so that, although you might be quite sure as to what he would do, you were never as safe as to what he would say; wherefore to know him a little was to dislike him, but to know him well was to love him. There was a liking between him and Wholesome, but each was more or less a source of wonderment to the other. Nor was it long before I saw that both these men were patient lovers in their way of the quiet and pretty Quaker dame who ruled over our little household, though to the elder man, Mr. Schmidt, she was a being at whose feet he laid a homage which he felt to be hopeless of result, while he was schooled by sorrowful fortunes to accept the position as one which he hardly even wished to change.

It was on a warm sunny morning very early, for we were up and away betimes, that Mr. Schmidt and I and Wholesome took our first walk together through the old market-sheds. We turned into Market Street at Fourth Street, whence the sheds ran downwards to the Delaware. The pictures they gave me to store away in my mind are all of them vivid enough, but none more so than that which I saw with my two friends on the first morning when we wandered through them together.

On either side of the street the farmers' wagons stood backed up against the sidewalk, each making a cheap shop, by which stood the sturdy owners under the trees, laughing and chaffering with their customers. We ourselves turned aside and walked down the centre of the street under the sheds. On either side at the entry of the market, odd business was being plied, the traders being mostly colored women with bright chintz dresses and richly-tinted bandanna handkerchiefs coiled turban-like above their dark faces. There were rows of roses in red pots, and venders of marsh calamus, and "Hot corn, sah, smokin' hot," and "Pepper-pot, bery nice," and sellers of horse-radish and snapping-turtles, and of doughnuts dear to grammar-school lads. Within the market was a crowd of gentlefolks, followed by their black servants with baskets,—the elderly men in white or gray stockings, with knee-buckles, the younger in very tight nankeen breeches and pumps, frilled shirts, and ample cravats, and long blue swallow-tailed coats with brass buttons. Ladies whose grandchildren go no more to market were there in gowns with strangely short waists and broad gypsy bonnets, with the flaps tied down by wide ribbons over the ears. It was a busy and good-humored throng.

"Ah," said Schmidt, "what color!" and he stood quite wrapped in the joy it gave him looking at the piles of fruit, where the level morning sunlight, broken by the moving crowd, fell on great heaps of dark-green watermelons and rough cantaloupes, and warmed the wealth of peaches piled on trays backed by red rows of what were then called love-apples, and are now known as tomatoes; while below the royal yellow of vast overgrown pumpkins seemed to have set the long summer sunshine in their golden cheeks.

"If these were mine," said Schmidt, "I could not forever sell them. What pleasure to see them grow and steal to themselves such sweet colors out of the rainbow which is in the light!"

"Thee would make a poor gardener," said Wholesome, "sitting on thy fence in the sun and watching thy pumpkins,—damn nasty things anyhow!"

I looked up amazed at the oath, but Schmidt did not seem to remark it, and went on with us, lingering here and there to please himself with the lovely contrasts of the autumn fruit.

"Curious man is Schmidt," remarked Wholesome as we passed along. "I could wish thee had seen him when we took him this way first. Old Betsey, yonder, sells magnolia flowers in June, and also pond-lilies, which thee may know as reasonably pleasant things to thee or me; but of a sudden I find our friend Schmidt kneeling on the pavement with his head over a tub of these flowers, and every one around much amazed."

"Was it not seemly?" said Schmidt, joining us. "There are those who like music, but to me what music is there like the great attunement of color? and mayhap no race can in this rise over our black artists hereabout the market-ends."

"Thee is crazed of many colors," said Wholesome, laughing,—"a bull of but one."

Schmidt stopped short, to Wholesome's disgust. "What," said he, quite forgetful of the crowd, "is more cordial than color? This he recalleth was a woman black as night, with a red turban and a lapful of magnolias, and to one side red crabs in a basket, and to one side a tubful of lilies. Moss all about, I remember."

"Come along," said Wholesome. "The man is cracked, and in sunny weather the crack widens."

And so we went away down street to our several tasks, chatting and amused.

Those were most happy days for me, and I found at evening one of my greatest pleasures when Schmidt called for me after our early tea and we would stroll together down to the Delaware, where the great India ships lay at wharves covered with casks of madeira and boxes of tea and spices. Then we would put out in his little row-boat and pull away toward Jersey, and, after a plunge in the river at Cooper's Point, would lazily row back again while the spire of Christ Church grew dim against the fading sunset, and the lights would begin to show here and there in the long line of sombre houses. By this time we had grown to be sure friends, and a little help from me at a moment when I chanced to guess that he wanted money had made the bond yet stronger. So it came that he talked to me, though I was but a lad, with a curious freedom, which very soon opened to me a full knowledge of those with whom I lived.

One evening, when we had been drifting silently with the tide, he suddenly said aloud, "A lion in the fleece of the sheep."

"What?" said I, laughing.

"I was thinking of Wholesome," he replied. "But you do not know him. Yet he has that in his countenance which would betray a more cunning creature."

"How so?" I urged, being eager to know more of the man who wore the garb and tongue of Penn, and could swear roundly when moved.

"If it will amuse," said the German, "I will tell you what it befell me to hear to-day, being come into the parlor when Mistress White and Wholesome were in the garden, of themselves lonely."

"Do you mean," said I, "that you listened when they did not know of your being there?"

"And why not?" he replied. "It did interest me, and to them only good might come."

"But," said I, "it was not——"

"Well?" he added, as I paused, "——'Was not honor,' you were going to say to me. And why not? I obey my nature, which is more curious than stocked with honor. I did listen."

"And what did you hear?" said I.

"Ah, hear!" he answered. "What better is the receiver than is the thief? Well, then, if you will share my stolen goods, you shall know, and I will tell you as I heard, my memory being good."

"But——" said I.

"Too late; you stop me," he added: "you must hear now."

The scene which he went on to sketch was to me strange and curious, nor could I have thought he could give so perfect a rendering of the language, and even the accent, of the two speakers. It was also a revelation of the man himself, and he seemed to enjoy his power, and yet to suffer in the telling, without perhaps being fully conscious of it. The oars dropped from his hands and fell in against the thwarts of the boat, and he clasped his knees and looked up as he talked, not regarding at all his single, silent listener.

"When this is to be put upon the stage there shall be a garden and two personages."

"Also," said I, "a jealous listener behind the scenes."

"If you please," he said promptly, and plunged at once into the dialogue he had overheard:

"'Richard, thee may never again say the words which thee has said to me to-night. There is, thee knows, that between us which is builded up like as a wall to keep us the one from the other.'

"'But men and women change, and a wall crumbles, or thee knows it may be made to. Years have gone away, and the man who stole from thee thy promise may be dead, for all thee knows.'

"'Hush! thee causes me to see him, and though the dead rise not here, I am some way assured he is not yet dead, and may come and say to me "'Cilla,"—that is what he called me,—"thee remembers the night and thy promise, and the lightning all around us, and who took thee to shore from the wrecked packet on the Bulkhead Bar." The life he saved I promised.'

"'Well, and thee knows—— By Heaven! you well enough know who tortured the life he gave,—who robbed you,—who grew to be a mean sot, and went away and left you; and to such you hold, with such keep faith, and wear out the sweetness of life waiting for him!'

"'Richard!'

"'Have I also not waited, and given up for thee a life, a career,—little to give. I hope thee knows I feel that. Has thee no limit, Priscilla? Thee knows —God help me! how well you know—I love you. The world, the old world of war and venture, pulls at me always. Will not you find it worth while to put out a hand of help? Would it not be God taking your hand and putting it in mine?'

"'Thee knows I love thee.'

"'And if the devil sent him back to curse you anew——'

"'Shame, Richard! I would say, the Lord who layeth out for each his way, has 'pointed mine.'

"'And I?'

"'Thee would continue in goodness, loving me as a sister hardly tried.'

"'By God! I should go away to sea.'

"'Richard!'

"Which is the last word of this scene," added Schmidt. "You mayhap have about you punk and flint and steel."

I struck a light in silence, feeling moved by the story of the hurt hearts of these good people, and wondering at the man and his tale. Then I said, "Was that all?"

"Could you, if not a boy, ask me to say more of it? Light thy pipe and hold thy peace. Happy those who think not of women. I, who have for a hearth-side only the fire of an honest pipe—— 'Way there, my lad! pull us in and forget what a loose tongue and a soft summer night have given thee to hear from a silly old German who is grown weak of head and sore at soul. How the lights twinkle!"

Had I felt any doubt at all of the truth of his narration, I should have ceased to do so when, for the next few days, I watched Mr. Wholesome, and saw him, while off his guard, looking at Mistress White askance with a certain wistful sadness, as of a great honest dog somehow hurt and stricken.

When an India ship came in, the great casks of madeira, southside, grape juice, bual, and what not were rolled away into the deep cellars of the India houses on the wharves, and left to purge their vinous consciences of such perilous stuff as was shaken up from their depths during the long homeward voyage. Then, when a couple of months had gone by, it was a custom for the merchant to summon a few old gentlemen to a solemn tasting of the wines old and new. Of this, Mr. Wholesome told me one day, and thought I had better remain to go through the cellars and drive out the bungs and drop in the testers, and the like. "I will also stay with thee," he added, "knowing perhaps better than thee the prices."

I learned afterward that Wholesome always stayed on these occasions, and I had reason to be glad that I too was asked to stay, for, as it chanced, it gave me a further insight into the character of my friend the junior partner.

I recall well the long cellar running far back under Water Street, with its rows of great casks, of which Wholesome and I started the bungs while awaiting the new-comers. Presently came slowly down the cellar-steps our senior partner in nankeen shanks, silk stockings, and pumps,—a frosty-visaged old man, with a nose which had fully earned the right to be called bottle. Behind him limped our old porter in a blue check apron. He went round the cellar, and at every second cask, having lighted a candle, he held it upside down until the grease had fallen thick on the cask, and then turning the candle stuck it fast in its little pile of tallow, so that by and by the cellar was pretty well lighted. Presently, in groups or singly, came old and middle-aged gentlemen, and with the last our friend Schmidt, who wandered off to a corner and sat on a barrel-head watching the effects of the mingling of daylight and candlelight, and amused in his quiet way at the scene and the intense interest of the chief actors in it, which, like other things he did not comprehend, had for him the charm of oddness. I went over and stood by him while the porter dropped the testerglass into the cool depths of cask after cask, and solemn counsel was held and grave decisions reached. I was enchanted with one meagre, little old gentleman of frail and refined figure, who bent over his wine with closed eyes, as if to shut out all the sense-impressions he did not need, while the rest waited to hear what he had to say.

"Needs a milk fining," muttered the old gentleman, with eyes shut as if in prayer.

"Wants its back broke with a good lot of eggshell," said a short, stout man with a snuff-colored coat, the collar of which came well up the back of his head.

"Ach!" murmured Schmidt. "The back to be hurt with eggshell! What will he say with that?"

"Pshaw!" said a third: "give it a little rest, and then the white of an egg to every five gallons. Is it bual?"

"Is it gruel?" said our senior sarcastically.

"Wants age. A good wine for one's grandchildren," murmured my old friend with shut eyes.

"What is it he calls gruel?" whispered Schmidt. "How nice is a picture he makes when he shuts his eyes and the light of the candle comes through the wine, all bright ruby, in the dark here! And ah, what is that?" for Wholesome, who had been taking his wine in a kindly way, and having his say with that sense of being always sure which an old taster affects, glancing out of one of the little barred cellar-windows which looked out over the wharf, said abruptly, "Ha! ha! that won't do!"

Turning, I saw under the broad-brimmed hat in the clear gray eyes a sudden sparkle of excitement as he ran hastily up the cellar-stairs. Seeing that something unusual was afloat, I followed him quickly out on to the wharf, where presently the cause of his movement was made plain.

Beside the wharf was a large ship, with two planks running down from her decks to the wharf. Just at the top of the farther one from us a large black-haired, swarthy man was brutally kicking an aged negro, who was hastily moving downward, clinging to the hand-rail. Colored folks were then apt to be old servants,—that is to say, friends,—and this was our pensioned porter, old Tom. I was close behind Wholesome at the door of the counting-house. I am almost sure he said "Damnation!" At all events, he threw down his hat, and in a moment was away up the nearer plank to the ship's deck, followed by me. Meanwhile, however, the black and his pursuer had reached the wharf, where the negro, stumbling and still clinging to the rail, was seized by the man who had struck him. In the short struggle which ensued the plank was pulled away from the ship's side, and fell just as Wholesome was about to move down it. He uttered an oath, caught at a loose rope which hung from a yard, tried it to see if it was fast, went up it hand over hand a few feet, set a foot on the bulwarks, and swung himself fiercely back across the ship, and then, with the force thus gained, flew far in air above the wharf, and dropping lightly

on to a pile of hogsheads, leapt without a word to
the ground, and struck out with easy power at the
man he sought, who fell as if a butcher's mallet had
stunned him,—fell, and lay as one dead. The whole
action would have been amazing in any man, but to
see a Quaker thus suddenly shed his false skin and
come out the true man he was, was altogether bewildering,—the more so for the easy grace with
which the feat was done. Everybody ran forward,
while Wholesome stood, a strange picture, his eyes
wide open and his pupils dilated, his face flushed and
lips a little apart, showing his set white teeth while
he awaited his foe. Then, as the man rallied and sat
up, staring wildly, Wholesome ran forward and looked
at him, waving the crowd aside. In a moment, as
the man rose still bewildered, his gaze fell on Wholesome, and, growing suddenly white, he sat down on
a bundle of staves, saying faintly, "Take him away!
Don't let him come near!"

"Coward!" said I; "one might have guessed that."

"There is to him," said Schmidt at my elbow,
"some great mortal fear; the soul is struck."

"Yes," said Wholesome, "the soul is struck.
Some one help him,"—for the man had fallen over
in something like a fit,—and so saying strode away,
thoughtful and disturbed in face, as one who had
seen a ghost.

As he entered the counting-house through the
group of dignified old merchants, who had come out
to see what it all meant, one of them said, "Pretty
well for a Quaker, Friend Richard!"

Wholesome did not seem to hear him, but walked

in, drank a glass of wine which stood on a table, and sat down silently.

"Not the first feat of that kind he has done," said the elder of the wine-tasters.

"No," said a sea-captain near by. "He boarded the Penelope in that fashion during the war, and as he lit on her deck cleared a space with his cutlass till the boarding-party joined him."

"With his cutlass?" said I. "Then he was not always a Quaker?"

"No," said our senior; "they don't learn these gymnastics at Fourth and Arch, though perchance the overseers may have a word to say about it."

"Quaker or not," said the wine-taster, "I wish any of you had legs as good or a heart as sound. Very good body, not too old, and none the worse for a Quaker fining."

"That's the longest sentence I ever heard Wilton speak," said a young fellow aside to me; "and, by Jove! he is right."

I went back into the counting-house and was struck with the grim sadness of face of our junior partner. He had taken up a paper and affected to be reading, but, as I saw, was staring into space. Our senior said something to him about Old Tom, but he answered in an absent way, as one who half hears or half heeds. In a few moments he looked up at the clock, which was on the stroke of twelve, and seeing me ready, hat in hand, to return home for our one-o'clock dinner, he gathered himself up, as it were, limb by limb, and taking his wide-brimmed hat brushed it absently with his sleeve. Then he looked at it a moment with a half smile, put it on decisively and went out and away up Arch Street with swifter and swifter strides. By and by he said, "You do not walk as well as usual."

"But," said I, "no one could keep up with you."

"Do not try to; leave a sore man to nurse his hurts. I suppose you saw my folly on the wharf,— saw how I forgot myself?"

"Ach!" said Schmidt, who had toiled after us hot and red, and who now slipped his quaint form in between us; "Ach! 'You forgot yourself.' This say you? I do think you did remember your true self for a time this morning."

"Hush! I am a man ashamed. Let us talk no more of it. I have ill kept my faith," returned Wholesome, impatiently.

"You may believe God doth not honor an honest man," said Schmidt; "which is perhaps a God Quaker, not the God I see to myself."

I had so far kept my peace, noting the bitter self-reproach of Wholesome, and having a lad's shyness before an older man's calamity; but now I said indignantly, "If it be Friends' creed to see the poor and old and feeble hurt without raising a hand, let us pray to be saved from such religion."

"But," said Wholesome, "I should have spoken to him in kindness first. Now I have only made of him a worse beast, and taught him more hatred. And he of all men!"

"There is much salvation in some mistakes," said Schmidt, smiling.

Just then we were stopped by two middle-aged

Friends in drab of orthodox tint, from which nowadays Friends have much fallen away into gay browns. They asked a question or two about an insurance on one of our ships; and then the elder said, "Thy hand seems bleeding, Friend Richard;" which was true; he had cut his knuckles on his opponent's teeth, and around them had hastily wrapped a handkerchief which showed stains of blood here and there.

"Ach!" said Schmidt, hastening to save his friend annoyance. "He ran against something. And how late is it! Let us go."

But Wholesome, who would have no man lie ever so little for his benefit, said quietly, "I hurt it knocking a man down;" and now for the first time to-day I observed the old amused look steal over his handsome face and set it a-twitching with some sense of humor as he saw the shock which went over the faces of the two elders when we bade them good-morning and turned away.

Wholesome walked on quickly, and as it seemed plain that he would be alone, we dropped behind.

"What is all this?" said I. "Does a man grieve thus because he chastises a scoundrel?"

"No," said Schmidt. "The Friend Wholesome was, as you may never yet know, an officer of the navy, and when your war being done he comes here, there is a beautiful woman whom he must fall to loving, and this with some men being a grave disorder, he must go and spoil a good natural man with the clothes of a Quaker, seeing that what the woman did was good in his sight."

"But," said I, "I don't understand."

"No," said he; "yet you have read of Eve and Adam. Sometimes they give us good apples and sometimes bad. This was a russet, as it were, and at times the apple disagrees with him for that with the new apple he got not a new stomach."

I laughed a little, but said, "This is not all. There was something between him and the man he struck which we do not yet know. Did you see him?"

"Yes, and before this,—last week some time in the market-place. He was looking at Old Dinah's tub of white lilies when I noticed him, and to me came a curious thinking of how he was so unlike them, many people having for me flower-likeness, and this man, being of a yellow swarthiness and squat-browed, minded me soon of the toadstool you call a corpse-light."

"Perhaps we shall know some time; but here is home, and will he speak of it to Mistress White, do you think?"

"Not ever, I suppose," said Schmidt; and we went in.

The sight we saw troubled me. In the little back parlor, at a round mahogany table with scrolled edges and claw toes sat facing the light Mistress White. She was clad in a gray silk with tight sleeves, and her profusion of rich chestnut hair, with its wilful curliness that forbade it to be smooth on her temples, was coiled in a great knot at the back of her head. Its double tints and strange changefulness, and the smooth creamy cheeks with their moving islets of roses that would come and go at a word, were pretty protests of Nature, I used to think, against the demure tints of her pearl-gray silken gown. She was looking out into the garden, quite heedless of the older dame, who sat as her wont was between the windows, and chirruped now and then, mechanically, " Has thee a four-leaved clover ?" As I learned some time after, one of our older clerks, perhaps with a little malice of self-comfort at the fall of his senior's principles, had, on coming home, told her laughingly all the story of the morning. Perhaps one should be a woman and a Friend to enter into her feelings. She was tied by a promise and by a sense of personal pledge to a low and disgraced man, and then coming to love another despite herself she had grown greatly to honor him. She might reason as she would that only a sense of right and a yearning for the fulness of a righteous life had made him give up his profession and fellows, and turn aside to follow the harder creed of Fox, but she well knew with a woman's keenness of view that she herself had gone for something in this change; and now, as sometimes before, she reproached herself with his failures. As we came in she hastily dried her eyes and went out of the room. At dinner little was said, but in the afternoon there was a scene of which I came to know all a good while later.

Some of us had gone back to the afternoon work when Mr. Wholesome, who had lingered behind, strayed thoughtfully into the little back garden. There under a thin-leaved apricot tree sat Mistress White, very pretty, with her long fair fingers clasped over a book which lay face down on her lap. Presently she was aware of Richard Wholesome walking to and fro and smoking a long-stemmed clay pipe, then, as yet in England, called a churchwarden. These were two more than commonly good-looking persons, come of sturdy English stock, fined down by that in this climate which has taken the coarseness of line and feature out of so many of our broods, and has made more than one English painter regret that the Vandyke faces had crossed the ocean to return no more.

Schmidt and I looked out a moment into the long vista where, between the rose-boughs bending from either wall under the apricot, we could see the gray silvery shimmer of the woman's dress, and beyond it, passing to and fro, the broad shoulders of the ex-captain.

"Come," I said, "walk down with me to the wharf."

"Yet leave me," he returned. "I shall wisely do to sit here on the step over the council-fire of my pipe. Besides, when there are not markets and flowers, and only a strait-down, early-afternoon sun, I shall find it a more noble usage of time to see of my drama another scene. The actors are good;" and he pointed with his pipe-stem down to the garden. "And this," he said, "is the mute chorus of the play," indicating a kitten which had made prey of the grand-dame's ball of worsted, and was rolling it here and there with delight.

"But," I answered, "it is not right or decent to spy upon others' actions."

"For right!" he said. "Ach! what I find right to me is my right; and for decent, I understand you not. But if I tell you what is true, I find my pleasure to sit here and see the maiden when at times the winds pull up the curtain of the leaves."

"Well! well!" said I, for most of the time he was not altogether plain as to what he meant, as when he spoke of the cat as a chorus. "Well! well! you will go out with me on the water at sundown?"

"That may be," he answered; and I went away.

I have observed since then, in the long life I have lived, that the passion called love, when it is a hopeless one, acts on men as ferments do on fluids after their kind,—turning some to honest wine and some to vinegar. With our stout little German all trials seemed to be of the former use, so that he took no ill from those hurts and bruises which leave other men sore and tender. Indeed, he talked of Mistress White to me, or even to Wholesome, whom he much embarrassed, in a calm, half-amused way, as of a venture which he had made, and, having failed, found it pleasant to look back upon as an experience not altogether to be regretted. We none of us knew until much later that it was more than a mere fancy for a woman who was altogether so sweet and winsome that no man needed an excuse for loving her. When by and by I also came to love a good woman, I used to try myself by the measure of this man's lack of self-love, and wonder how he could have seen with good-will the woman he cared for come to like another man better. This utter sweetness of soul has ever been to me a riddle.

An hour passed by, when Schmidt heard a footfall

in the room behind him, and rising saw an old member of the Society of Friends who came at times to our house, and was indeed trustee of a small estate which belonged to Mistress White. Nicholas Oldmixon was an overseer in the Fourth Street meeting, and much looked up to among Friends as a prompt and vigilant guardian of their discipline. Perhaps he would have been surprised to be told that he had that in his nature which made the post of official fault-finder agreeable; but so it was, I fancy, and he was here on such an errand. The asceticism of Friends in those days, and the extent to which Mr. Oldmixon, like the more strict of his sect, carried his views as to gravity of manner and the absence of color in dress and furniture, were especially hateful to Schmidt, who lived and was happy in a region of color and sentiment and gayety. Both, I doubt not, were good men, but each was by nature and training altogether unable to sympathize with the other.

"Good-evening!" said Schmidt, keeping his seat in the low window-sill.

Mr. Oldmixon returned, "Thee is well, I trust?"

"Ach! with such a sun and the last roses, which seem the most sweet, and these most lovely of fall-flowers, and a good book and a pipe," said Schmidt, "who will not be well? Have you the honest blessing of being a smoker?"

"Nay," said the Quaker, with evident guarding of his words. "Thee will not take it amiss should I say it is a vain waste of time?"

"But," answered Schmidt, "time hath many uses.

The one is to be wasted; and this a pipe mightily helps. I did think once, when I went to meeting, how much more solemn it would be for each man to have a pipe to excuse his silence."

"Thee jests idly, I fear," said the Friend, coloring, and evidently holding himself in check. "Is that friend Wholesome in the garden? I have need to see him."

"Yea," said Schmidt, with a broad smile, "he is yonder under a tree, like Adam in the garden. Let us take a peep at Paradise."

Mr. Oldmixon held his peace, and walked quietly out of the window and down the gravelled path. There were some who surmised that his years and his remembrance of the three wives he had outlived did not altogether suffice to put away from him a strong sentiment of the sweetness of his ward. Perhaps it was this notion which lit up with mirth the ruddy face of the German as he walked down the garden behind the slim ascetic figure of the overseer of meeting in his broad hat and drab clothes. On the way the German plucked a dozen scarlet roses, a late geranium or two, and a few leaves of motley Poinsetta.

Wholesome paused a moment to greet the newcomer quietly, and straightway betook himself absently to his walk again to and fro across the garden. Mistress White would have had the old overseer take her seat, but this he would not do. He stood a moment near her, as if irresolute, while Schmidt threw himself down on the sward, and, half turning over, tossed roses into the gray lap of Mistress

White, saying, "How prettily the God of heaven has dressed them!"

Mistress White took up the flowers, not answering the challenge, but glancing under her long lashes at the ex-captain, to whom presently the overseer turned, saying, "Would thee give me a word or two with thee by ourselves, Richard?"

"There are none in the parlor," said Priscilla, "if thee will talk there."

"If," said Wholesome, "it be of business, let it wait till to-morrow, and I will call upon thee: I am not altogether myself to-day."

"Nay," said Nicholas, gathering himself up a little, "thee must know theeself that I would not come to thee here for business: thee knows my exactness in such matters."

"And for what, then, are you come?" said Wholesome, with unusual abruptness.

"For speech of that in thy conduct which were better, as between an elder Friend and a younger, to be talked over alone," said Mr. Oldmixon, severely.

Now, Wholesome, though disgusted by his lack of power to keep the silent pledges he had given when he entered the Society of Friends, was not dissatisfied with his conduct as judged by his own standard of right. Moreover, like many warm-hearted people, he was quick of temper, as we have seen. His face flushed, and he paused beside the overseer: "There are none here who do not know most of what passed this morning; but as you do not know all, let me advise you to hold your peace and go your ways, and leave me to such reproach as God may send me."

"If that God send thee any," muttered Schmidt.

But Nicholas Oldmixon was like a war-horse smelling the battle afar off, and anything like resistance to an overseer in the way of duty roused him into the sternness which by no means belonged to the office, but rather to the man. "If," he said, "any in membership with us do countenance or promote tumults, they shall be dealt with as disorderly persons. Wherefore did thee give way to rash violence this morning?"

Priscilla grew pale. "I think," she said, "Friend Nicholas, thee forgets the Christian courtesy of our people one to another. Let it rest a while; friend Richard may come to think better of it by and by."

"And that I trust he may never," muttered Schmidt.

But the overseer was not to be stayed. "Thee would do better to mind the things of thy house and leave us," he said. "The ways of this young man have been more than once a scandal, and are like to come before the meeting to be dealt with."

"Sir," returned Wholesome, approaching him and quite forgetting his plain speech to make it plainer, "your manners do little credit to your age or your place. Listen: I told you to speak no more of this matter;" and he seized him by the lappel of his coat and drew him aside a few paces. "For your own sake, I mean. Let it die out, with no more of talk or nonsense."

"For my sake!" exclaimed the overseer; "and why? Most surely thee forgets theeself."

i

"For your own sake," said Wholesome, drawing him still farther away, and bending toward him, so that his words were lost to Schmidt and Priscilla, "and for your son John's. It was he whom I struck to-day."

Mr. Oldmixon grew white and staggered as if stricken. "Why did thee not come and tell me?" he said. "It had been kinder; and where is that unhappy man?"

"I do not know," returned Wholesome.

"Nevertheless, be it he or another, thee was in the wrong, and I have done my duty. And is my unhappy son yet alive?" and so saying, he turned away, and without other words walked through the house with uncertain steps and went down the street, while Wholesome, with softened face, watched him from the doorstep. Then he went back quietly into the garden, and turning to Schmidt, said, "Will you oblige me by leaving me with Mistress White? I will explain to thee by and by."

Schmidt looked up surprised, but seeing how pale and stern he looked, rose and went into the house. The woman turned expectant.

"Priscilla, the time has come when thee must choose between me and him."

"He has come back? I always knew he would come."

"Yes, he has come back; I saw him to-day," said Wholesome, "and the John Oldmixon of to-day is more than ever cruel and brutal. Will thee trust me to make thee believe that?"

"I believe thee," she returned; "but because he is

this and worse, shall I forget my word or turn aside from that which, if bitter for me, may save his soul alive?"

"And yet you love me?"

"Have I not said so?" she murmured, with a half smile.

The young man came closer and seized both hands in his: "Will it not be a greater sin, loving me, to marry him?"

"But he may never ask me, and then I shall wait, for I had better die fit in soul to be thy wife than come to thee unworthy of a good man's love."

He dropped her hands and moved slowly away, she watching him with full eyes. Then he turned and said, "But should he fall—fall as he must—and come to be what his life will surely make him, a felon whom no woman could marry——"

"Thee makes duty hard for me, Richard," she answered. "Do not make me think thee cruel. When in God's good time he shall send me back the words of promise I wrote when he went away a disgraced man, to whom, nevertheless, I owed my life, then—— Oh, Richard, I love thee! Do not hurt me. Pray for me and him."

"God help us!" he said. "We have great need to be helped;" and suddenly leaning over he kissed her forehead for the first time, and went away up the garden and into the house.

The soft September days were past, and the crisp October freshness was with us before my little drama went a step further. Wholesome had got into a fashion of seeking loneliness, and thus Schmidt and

I were more than ever thrown together. So it came that on a Saturday,—which to me, a somewhat privileged person in the counting-house, was always a half-holiday,—and on Sunday afternoon, if I went not to Christ Church, we were wont to wander at will about the lovely country along the Schuylkill or up the Wissahickon talking of many things. Nor did Schmidt ever tire of the crowded market-place, and although in our walks he talked of what he saw there and elsewhere as with a child's pleasure in his own thoughts and words, they never wearied me. To many he was more odd than pleasant, because on all subjects and at all times he turned himself inside out, with little regard to what he had to say or who heard him. I recall well some of our morning strolls.

"Let us walk serenely," he said. (I suppose he meant slowly enough to think.) "The Wholesome goes before, and with what a liberal strength he walks! How beautiful to see! As if he would give away his legs when he walks, so much is there of strength he needs not in the Quaker life."

"I cannot see yet," I said, "why he must turn Quaker. I would have trusted that man with untold gold or a woman's honor the first half-hour he talked to me."

"I like not that sect," returned Schmidt. "It does make nicer women than men. Should there be two religions for the two sexes? and do you think ever Penn and Mr. Fox did take among the women a vote when they went to the queerness of robe which is theirs?"

"I have heard," I said, "that it is only a continuance of the plainer fashions of their own time."

"And why," he said, "should to-day wear the garments of a century away? And does not Nature mock their foolish customs? Even now behold how pretty a sight is this." And he paused before a stall where the ripe Spanish watermelons split into halves showed their gorgeous red. "How spendthrift is Nature of her tints! and in the peach-time there is a pleasure to eat of this scarlet! I thought it so pretty last week when we dined with Mr. Wilton,—the red melons on the shining brown mahogany, and the gray-greens of the apples, and the Heath peaches, soft and rosy, with the ruby of the madeira wine. How charming a thing is a table after dinner what few do ever think!"

"Stop!" I said: "look there!" A little way before us, in simple tints of gray serge, and with rebel curls peeping out under her stiff, ugly silk bonnet, Priscilla was moving down the market. She was busy with her daily marketing, and behind or beside her was our old brown Nancy, trim and cleanly, with her half-filled basket. A few steps in the rear was a man who paused and held back as she stopped, and then went on. As I caught his side face and hungry eyes, and a certain hyena-like swiftness of impatient movement, I knew him for the man whom Wholesome had struck on the wharf a few weeks before. Now he was clad in the height of the fashion, with striped silken hose, tight nankeen breeches, a brown swallow-tailed coat, and an ample cambric cravat. The bright brass buttons were new, the beaver hat, scroll-rimmed and broad on top, was faultlessly brushed.

"Ach!" said Schmidt, "a devil which is handsome for little of good! The plainer parent must have been made to be liberal of money to plume the fine bird."

Just then the man looked round, and, Wholesome being gone on ahead, and seeing no one he knew, he paused beside Priscilla and spoke to her. What he said we did not hear. She turned, a little startled, and dropped her purse. The man set his foot on it, and stooping as if to look for it, deftly picked it up and slipped it into his pocket.

I started forward.

"Nay," said Schmidt, "the audience shall not spoil the play. Wait."

Her face grew pale, and I at least thought she saw but would not notice the mean theft. A few brief words passed between them. He asked something, and she hesitated, I thought. Then a few more words, and as we went by I heard her say something about the afternoon, and then with a word more he turned and left her.

"Also," said Schmidt, "the plot thickens. How handsome and foul he is, with that visage clean shaven and the nose of hawk! We shall see when all the performers are come upon the stage. Goodby! I go to see if further he will amuse me."

For my part, bewildered at Priscilla's knowledge of this ruffian, astonished at his gay change of dress, and recalling his emotion on the wharf, I also began to feel an interest in the drama going on about me.

After dinner next day, when her guests save myself had gone away to their several tasks, Mistress Priscilla in the garden grew busy among the roses with the dead leaves and the bugs. A very pretty picture she made, and if I had been a painter it is thus I should have wished to paint her. Against the wall of dark-red brick the long bending rose-branches made a briery hedge of green and leafy curves, flecked here and there with roses red, white, and pink; and against this background there was the charming outline of Priscilla in ashen-tinted silk, with a fine cambric handkerchief about her throat, and a paler silk kerchief pinned away from the neck on the shoulders, much as Friends wear them still. A frail pretence of a cap there was also, and wicked double tints of hair the color of chestnuts and dead leaves and buttonwood bark and such other pretty uncertain tints as have stored away a wealth of summer sun. Now and then she was up on tiptoe to pluck a rose or break off a dead stem, and then the full ripe curves of her figure were charming to see. And so, like a gray butterfly, she flitted round the garden-wall, and presently, quite in a natural way, came upon me demurely reading.

"Thee should be up and away to thy business, friend loiterer," she said.

"I think I shall stay at home this afternoon," I answered, giving no reason.

I saw she looked troubled, but in a moment she added, "Not if I wanted thee to do an errand for me in Front Street."

"I have a bone in my foot," said I, recalling one of our boy excuses for laziness.

"But I would pay thee with a rose and some thanks," she returned, laughing.

"No doubt that would pay some folks, but I am not to be bribed. If I were older it might answer; but as I am only a boy, I may tell you how pretty you look among the roses. And I think you are dressed for company this afternoon."

"Thee is a very saucy lad," she replied, half troubled, half smiling, "and—and—I must tell thee, I suppose, that I am looking for a friend to come on a business of mine, and I shall like thee better if thee will go away to-day, because——"

"Because why?" I said.

"Because I ask thee to go."

At this moment, as I rose to obey her, laughing and saying, "But will you not tell me his name?" Schmidt appeared in the window.

"Ah!" said he, smiling his pleased, quiet smile, which rarely grew into noisy mirth, "we masquerade of this pleasant afternoon as a queen of pearls. You would have lacked some one to admire you were I not come back so good luckily now."

Priscilla blushed, but said quickly, "This lazy boy has been saying much the same things. Ah!" and she looked worried of a sudden as the knocker sounded. "There!" she exclaimed, "some one is coming to see me—on business. Please to leave me the parlor."

"Ah, well!" said Schmidt, smiling, "we will go;' and he turned to enter the house.

"But not that way," she said hastily. "I—I am in trouble: I do not want you to see— I mean—

please to go out by the garden-gate: I will explain another time."

Schmidt looked surprised, but, taking my arm, went without more words down the garden, saying in my ear, in his queer jerky way, "Hast thou ever seen what a smear the slimy slug will make on the rose-leaf?"

I said, "I do not understand."

"But God does, my lad; and when thy rose comes, pray that there be no vile slugs afoot."

From that evening we all noticed a sad change in Priscilla. The gay sallies and coquetry which had defied all bonds were gone, and she went about her needed household work silent, preoccupied, and pale. The greatest charm of this woman was in her pretty little revolts against Quaker ways, and her endless sympathy with everybody's tastes and pursuits; but now she was utterly changed, until all of us who loved her, as friend or as more than friend, began to notice her sadness and to question among ourselves as to its cause.

It soon grew to be known among us that in the afternoons Priscilla had meetings at home with a stranger, and we observed also that Wholesome had become silent and abstracted. This was a source of some amusement to our little company of India clerks and supercargoes, who laid it to the fact that Wholesome's sad conduct having been brought to the consideration of the monthly meeting, the overseers had waited upon him and wasted much time in fruitless admonitions, the ex-captain proving quite unable to see that he had acted otherwise than became a God-fearing man. I suspect this treason to the creed of Friends sat easy on him, and graver by far were the other questions which beset him on every side.

At last, one afternoon early in October, Wholesome had started a little late for the counting-house, when, as we passed down Arch Street near Fifth, he suddenly stopped and said, "I must go back. This thing has gone on long enough. A man must put his hand in the business."

"What is it?" said I, surprised at the sternness of his manner.

"Do you see that person?" he replied, pointing to a fashionably-dressed gentleman on the far side of the way, going up the street with a certain leisurely swagger. It was the man he had struck on the wharf, and whom I had seen in the market-place.

I said, "Yes, I see him. What do you mean to do?"

"No matter. I am going home: I have stood this long enough."

"But what do you mean to do?"

"Kill him," said Wholesome, quietly.

I was at once shocked, alarmed, and a little amused, it seemed so incongruous a threat from a man in drab and broad-brim. But I had the sense to try to dissuade him from returning as we stood under the lindens, he cool and quiet, I anxious and troubled, as any man so young would have been. At last he broke away, saying, "I am going home. You need not come. I do not want you."

"If you go back," I said, "I go also."

"As you please," he returned; and we went swiftly homeward, without a word on either side.

Since then I have seen on the stage many and curious scenes, but none more dramatic than that on which the curtain rose at four o'clock on this pleasant October evening.

Wholesome, pale, cold-visaged, handsome, opened the door as if his being there were a matter of course, and walked into the back parlor. Between the windows, as usual, sat the older dame, of no more mortal consequence than a clock. On the window-step we saw Priscilla, and as we passed out of the nearer window into the garden, I observed our dark-visaged friend leaning against the window-jamb and talking earnestly to her.

She rose up, a little flurried and anxious, saying, "Perhaps thee remembers John Oldmixon, Richard? And these are Richard Wholesome and a new friend, Henry Shelburne."

As she spoke she scanned furtively and with a certain uneasiness the two strongly-contrasted faces. Neither man put out his hand, but Wholesome said, "Yes, I remember him, and well enough. He has not changed, I think;" and as he ended, his glance rose to meet the darker eyes of his foe. If will to hurt had been power to slay with the look which followed this silent challenge, there would have been a dead man at Priscilla's feet. John Oldmixon must have been well used to the eye of hate.

"Nay," he said, "we have shifted parts like men in a play I once saw. I went away a Quaker, and am come back a man of the world: you went away a gay midshipman, and here you are a Friend in drab."

"Yes, a Friend," said Priscilla, quickly, lifting her eyes to Wholesome's with mute pleading in their fulness.

"I suppose," said I, desirous to turn the talk from what seemed to me dangerous ground,—"I suppose there is no rule about Friends' dress, is there? Who sets the fashions for Friends?"

"There are none," she said, smiling. "Like the flowers of the field and the trees, our dress is ever the same."

"Ah," said Wholesome, who was getting his passion well in hand, "I think thee will see some new fall patterns in the leaves overhead, Priscilla. Thee has given us a weak example for Friends."

"It has little beauty," said Oldmixon, "this Friends' dress, but it may have its use, for all that. For instance, no one would insult or strike a man in drab, however great the provocation he might give. It is as good as chain-armor."

"Why not?" replied Wholesome, flushing. "A man may be a man, whatever his garb, and I, for one, should feel as free to chastise a scoundrel to-day as ten years ago, and as ready to answer him."

"Oh, Richard! Richard! thee forgets!"

"True," he said, "I did. I forgot you. Pardon me!"

"It is so easy to brag in drab," returned Oldmixon. "That's another of its uses. But that concerns no one here. Shall I see you to-morrow, Priscilla?"

The last insult quieted Wholesome, as such things

do quiet some men. He made no answer, but smiled and went away down the garden whistling,—a thing I had never heard him do before,—while Priscilla said in a half whisper, "No, not to-morrow. How can thee find it pleasing to annoy my friends? Does thee think that a thing I should like?"

"He is not *my* friend," replied the man, brutally, and losing his temper as easily with the woman as he had kept it with the man. "Folks who masquerade in Quaker clothes need to be taught lessons sometimes."

"Thee forgets thyself," said Priscilla. "Think a little, and take back thee words."

"Not I," said he, sneeringly. "A fellow like that wants a teacher at times."

Priscilla was a woman, and the man thus jeered at was out of earshot, and she loved him; so for once her creed and temper alike failed her, and she said proudly, "I hear it is thee rather that has been to school to him, and did not like thee lesson."

"By Heaven!" said he, angrily, "you are no better Quaker than he! I hope my wife will have better manners." He flushed with shame and with wrath at thus coming to learn that Priscilla knew of his humiliation. "Good-by!" he said, and turned to leave.

But Priscilla was herself again. "I beg of thee do not go in anger," she said. "I was wrong: pardon me!"

"Not I," he returned. "Think a little next time before you speak."

"John!" she said, reproachfully, but he was gone.

As he went I saw Wholesome pass quietly out of the garden-gate, and surmising that he had gone to meet Oldmixon, and not knowing what might come of it, I made some excuse, and leaving Priscilla pale and shaken, I followed by the front door.

I was right. As Oldmixon crossed Second Street, I walking behind him, Wholesome came out of a side lane and touched him on the shoulder. There was no woman now, and both men came out in their true colors.

Oldmixon turned. He looked uneasy, and, I thought, scared. "What do you want?" he said.

Wholesome turned to me: "This is no business of yours: leave us, Shelburne."

"Not now," I said.

"Well, as you please; but step out of earshot. I have something to say to this man which concerns only him and me."

Upon this I walked away, but as their voices rose I caught enough to surprise me.

Wholesome spoke to him quietly for several minutes. Then Oldmixon replied aloud, "And if I say no?"

"Then," said Wholesome, also raising his voice, "I will tell her all."

"And what good will it do?" answered the other, angrily. "Do you think I will release her? and do you think she will lie while I carry this?" and he touched his breast-pocket. "She may never marry me, but you, at least, will be no better off. It will only be said you told a pretty story, thinking to compass your own ends."

Almost without knowing it I drew nearer, unnoted by the two angry men.

"Yet I will do it," said Wholesome.

"You little know her: tell her and try it," said the other.

Wholesome paused. Then he said, "I believe you are right, or let us suppose you so. What is to stop me from delivering you to justice to-morrow,—to-day?"

The other smiled: "Just because, if you feel sure this woman will marry me, you love her too well to damn her husband quite utterly."

Wholesome laughed hoarsely, and said, "Don't count on my goodness in that kind of fashion. By Heaven! you have been nearer death within this last week or two than you dream of; and I should no more think twice about the lesser business of putting you out of the way of soiling better lives than about crushing a cockroach."

Oldmixon looked at him keenly, and no doubt made the reflection that had he meant to act he would have done so without warning. His face lit up as if he were about to speak. Then he changed his purpose, was silent a moment, and said, "Richard Wholesome, there has been enough bad blood between me and you already. Let it stop here. This woman is out of your reach, and always will be while I live. For her sake let us be at peace."

"Peace!" said Wholesome. "You would not believe it if I were to say that if she loved you, and you were any way worth loving, I would help you to marry her and go away not quite unhappy. But now,"—and his scorn grew uncontrollable,—" now, to talk of peace,—peace with a cur, with a creature who holds a pure woman by a girl's promise which he treats as a business contract,—peace with a man who trades on a woman's hope that she can drag him out of the mire of his vices! I wonder at my own self-restraint," he added, as the other fell back a step before his angry advance.

"Will you hear me?" said Oldmixon.

"Hear you? No," said Wholesome. "When you hear of me again, it will be through the sheriff."

"Ah, is it so really?" returned the other. "Have your way, then, and see what will come of it;" and so saying, he turned and went away.

Wholesome stood an instant, and then, looking up, said to me, "You here yet? I suppose you have heard enough to trouble you. Do me the kindness not to mention it. I did not mean the talk should have been a long one, and it had better have been elsewhere, but a man is not always his own master."

This I thought myself, but the upper streets of Philadelphia were in that day half country, the wayfarers scarce, save on the main highways. I said to him that I had heard a good deal of what was said, but did not fully understand it.

"No need to," he replied. "Forget it, my lad."

That evening late, as we sat at our window in the second story, Schmidt and I, we heard voices in the garden just below us, at first low, then louder.

"It is Priscilla and Wholesome, not yet gone away to sleep," said Schmidt. "What will he? There is a something which ever she asks and ever he will not. And if she would it ask of the other, which is me, there would be ways to do it, I warrant you, and that quickly. Canst hear, my boy?"

"Hear?" said I aloud, so as to disturb the couple below, who, however, were too intent to heed my warning. "Hear? What business have I with other people's affairs?" and so I coughed again lustily.

"Foolish imp! why shall you spoil my drama?" said Schmidt. "Never have you paid as I have to get an interest in them which play; and think what a rare piece you spoil, and how pretty, too, with this jealous lover on the balcony and the drab Romeo and Juliet in the moonshine beneath! See! what is it they speak? He says, 'Yes, you shall have your way.' And about what, my lord? Would you mind if that I go below to hear?"

"Now that," I said, "you shall not do."

"And wherefore should I tarry?" he returned. "Are my motives as the crystal to be seen through? And if I listen for ill, that is ill; and if I go to listen for good——"

"Good or ill," said I, "friend Schmidt, we do not do such things here."

"And there is to myself wonderment that it is so," he returned; "and as it is my conscience that will bleed, I go."

"Not so," said I, laughing, and began to hail Wholesome in the garden, and to ask him to throw me a cheroot.

As I called out the voices ceased, and Schmidt,

quite furious, exclaimed, "There is not so much of amusing in the life of gray and drab here as that an interest shall be taken out of it, and nevermore be missed. The thing you have done is unhuman."

Meanwhile, Wholesome had thrown up to me his cigar-case, and Priscilla had flitted into the house like a misty ghost through the moonlight.

The little I had heard that night, and what Schmidt had added as comment, and what Wholesome had said to Oldmixon, could not fail, of course, to make clear to me that here was a mystery which seemed to be growing deeper.

Meanwhile, our daily work went on, while Mistress White grew paler than her white kerchief, and went about her household tasks watched by loving and tender eyes. As I was a sort of extra clerk at our counting-house and received no salary, I went and came with more liberty than the rest; whence it chanced that sometimes I was at home when John Oldmixon paid his frequent afternoon visits. I liked the man little, and since his meeting with Wholesome less than ever. Once or twice I found Priscilla crying after he had gone; and this so moved me that I made up my mind to tell Schmidt, partly because I was curious, and partly because, with a boy's lack of knowledge of the perplexities of life, I hoped to find or hear of some escape for her. I was saved this need by an event which chanced a day or two later.

I came home early in the afternoon with Schmidt to get our rough clothes, as we meant to be gone a day or two down the river in his boat, and to sleep the first night at Chester or Marcus Hook. As we entered the parlor I heard a harsh voice saying roughly, "I will wait no longer. Be as good as your written pledge, or let me go and drift to the devil, as I shall. Only one person can save me."

Schmidt seized my arm and held me back at the door a moment, and I heard Priscilla say, "Can thee fail to see how ill I grow? Will thee not wait but a little while, John,—only a little? Richard has promised me thee shall take no hurt: thee knows he would not lie."

All this while, at brief intervals, like a scared bird who sees near her nest a serpent, the old lady from her seat between the windows kept sounding her one note: "Has thee a four-leaved clover?" in a voice shrill and feeble.

Meanwhile, I had turned away as Oldmixon replied to Priscilla, "Not a week longer,—not a week! You are lying to me in your heart, and you only just dare not lie with your lips."

This brutal speech was too much for Schmidt. "The man," he said, "which can this suffer should no more breathe the air of God;" and so saying went in abruptly.

As he entered, I being behind him, John Oldmixon, confused and wrathful, let go his rough hold on Priscilla's wrists and rose up, seeking to compose his disturbed features. The German walked straight up to him. "Not ever do we abuse women in this house," he said. "Go straightways out of it."

Oldmixon laughed. "How is this, 'Cilla?" he said.

"What is called a gentleman," said Schmidt, "he

is very mild to women. Talk your great talk to me who am a man: what need to shelter by a petticoat."

By this time Priscilla was her quiet self. "Hush, John!" she said. "You will both remember my aged mother."

"Has thee a four-leaved clover?" said the old dame.

"There is of you but a child," returned Schmidt to Priscilla softly: "the ways of foul things like this one you do not know. Leave us but a moment, and never shall he more trouble thy sweetness."

Oldmixon's face grew gray with rage. "Insolent little Dutchman!" he said.

"Hush!" again broke in Priscilla. "Speak not thus;" and turning to Schmidt, "This is my husband that shall be. How we may differ is for us alone. I pray thee to go away, and be angry no more for the cross that is to be borne by me with what patience the Lord shall help me to get."

"He does not help me to any patience," said Schmidt, "seeing these things; but if it be as you say, I go; but as for this man———"

"Well?" said Oldmixon.

"Come away, Schmidt," I exclaimed. "This is no business of yours. Come!"

"Yes, go," said Priscilla, anxiously, standing like an angel of peace between the two angry men.

"Let it then be so," said Schmidt, "for now."

"And for always," said she.

And we turned and went without more words.

Another week went by, when one morning Schmidt proposed to me that we should walk up the Schuylkill to the Falls; and as I was always glad of his company, we set out after our one-o'clock dinner. Where we walked by ponds and green fields and gardens the great city has come and left no spot unfilled; but now, as then, above Fairmount the river rolled broad between grassy hills and bold rocky points. We hailed a boatman just below Callowhill Street, and being set on the far side went away northward along the river-marge. It was lovely then: it is so to-day. We walked on, leaving above us on the bank the sloping lawns of Solitude, Sweetbrier's, Eaglesfield, and at last Belmont, and, now by the water-side and now under the overhanging catalpas of the "River Road," came at last to the "Falls." In those days a vast rock extended two-thirds of the way across from the west side, and so dammed up the waters that they broke in foam through the narrow gap on the east, and fell noisily about six feet in a hundred and fifty yards. The rock, I recall well, was full of potholes, and there was one known from its shape as Devil Foot. Of all this there is to-day nothing left, the dam at Fairmount having hidden it under water, but in those times the view from the rock took in a lovely sweep of river down to Peter's Island and far beyond it.

That was a day to remember, and it brought out all that was most curious and quaint and sincere in my German friend. It was mid-October, and a haze which was gray or gold as shade or sun prevailed lay moveless everywhere.

Said Schmidt to me, basking on the rock, "Have you learned yet to look with curiousness at this pretty Nature which for us dresses with nice changes all the days?"

His speech often puzzled me, and I said as much this time.

"It is my bad English which I have when I try not to talk my Spenser or my Shakespeare, to which I went to school. It was not a mystery I meant. I would but this say, that it is gainful of what is most sweet in living to have got that wise nearness of love to Nature. Well! and I am not yet understood? So let it be. When a music which pleases you is heard, is it that it fills up full your throat some way and overflows your eyes?"

I was ever sensitive to harmony, and could follow him now. I said, "Yes, there are songs which are most sweet to me,—which so move me that I scarce hear them willingly."

"Thus," he said, "I am stirred by the great orchestra of color which is here, but music I know not. How strange is that! And if," he said, "you were to shut your eyes, what is it in this loveliness would stay with you?"

"Oh, but," said I, "no one thing makes it lovely. It is not only color, but sounds, like this rush of water at our feet."

"It is as you say," replied Schmidt. "And what a sweet-tempered day, with a gray haziness and a not unkindly coolness to the air where the sun is not!"

"A day like Priscilla," I said, demurely.

"Yes," he replied, "that was well said,—like Priscilla. How lovely sad that is," he went on, "to see the leaves shiver in the wind and rain all reds and golds through the air! And do you see this picture behind us, where is that great green fir, and around it to the top, like a flame, the scarlet of your Virginia creeper? And below these firs on the ground is a carpet,—a carpet all colors near, and gray pinks to us far away; and under the maples what you call,—ach! the wild words which fail me,—fine broken-up gold and red bits. It is what you call stippled, I mean."

"And the curled leaves afloat," I said, "how pretty they are."

"And the brown sedges," he added, "and the crumpled brown ferns, and over them the great splendid masses of color, which do laugh at a painter!"

Then we were silent a while, and the blue smoke went up in spirals from Schmidt's meerschaum. At last he said, in his odd, abrupt way, "To talk helps to think. This is a strange coil we have about our good Priscilla. I have been going it over in my own mind."

"I understand it so little," said I, "that I am unable to help you. Can you tell me more of it than I know already?"

"And why not?" said Schmidt, frankly. "This is it——"

"But stop!" said I. "If it involves other folks' secrets, I do not want to know it."

"That is my business," returned Schmidt, deliberately filling his pipe. "What I do I settle with my own conscience if I have any; which I know not clearly. How amazing some day to be called to an account for it, and then to put hands in the moral pockets and say, 'Where is it?' Let me talk my dark thoughts out to daylight."

"Well, then," I said, laughing, "go on."

"And first of Oldmixon. There is, I have come to know, a black history of this man in the war. Our good Wholesome was in the way to help him with money, so much that to pay he could not. Then is there a not nice story of a shipwreck, and boats too full, and women which he would throw overboard or not take in from a sinking ship, and sharp words and a quarrel with Wholesome, and these followed by a stab in the darkness, and a good man over in a raging sea and no more seen of men."

"Good Heavens!" said I: "do you mean he stabbed Wholesome?"

"It is so," he replied.

"And then?" said I.

"Next," he said, "is some foul horror of women shrieking lonely on a vessel's deck over which go the wailing seas. But this Wholesome is by a miracle afloat for hours on a spar, and saved by a passing ship."

"But knowing all this," I said, "why does he not tell it and drive the wretch away?"

"Because," returned Schmidt, "there is another side,—of a little Quaker girl, the ward of Nicholas Oldmixon, who is on a time before this saved from great peril of fear more than of death by this man, John Oldmixon, and then such love between them as may be betwixt a fair woman and a foul man."

"But," said I, "this does not seem enough to make our present tangle."

"Assuredly never," he went on. "But also the man takes to worse ways, and to the woman's girl-love comes later her belief that here is a soul to save. And, come what will, she, when he has fled away, writes letters in which she makes foolish promise to marry him when he comes back."

"But will she keep such an absurd promise?" I said.

"Is she a woman?" he answered. "There is a creature mingled of angel and fool which will do this thing, and let no man stop her."

"But," I added, "you have not told me why Wholesome does not go to the recorder and tell his story, and have the scoundrel arrested."

"Ah, true!" he said. "A day more and the thing would have been; but the beast, well warned by our foolish Quaker war-man, goes swiftly to Priscilla and is penitent over again, and will she save him?"

"And then?" said I.

"This Quaker woman turns my man Wholesome her finger around, and says, 'God has set me the task to marry this man, John Oldmixon, and save his soul alive,'—whatever that may mean,—and so she has Wholesome's good promise that he will leave the wretch to her and his conscience forever."

"And so it ends," said I, "and Priscilla is a dead woman. If I were Wholesome, I would save her despite herself, even if she never married me."

"But you are not Richard Wholesome," he returned. "There is half of him Quaker and half a brave gentleman, and all of him the bond-slave of a woman's foolish will."

"Then is it a tale told?" I said.

"Hardly do I know," replied Schmidt, rising. "There are two ends to all things. Let us go: the twilight falls, and how lovely is the golden light on the yellow hickories yonder!"

And so we strolled homeward lazily, the chill October evening air growing damper and the twilight well upon us before we reached the city.

Just as we were come to our own door, Schmidt, who had been long silent, stopped me and said, "There is a thing I would say to you for lack of an elder to listen. But first make me a promise that no man's ear shall get the value of what I have said to you."

"I will tell no one," I answered.

Then he paused: "This more I want of you. I have much weighed it before I thought to put on one so young what may come to be a burden; but also there is none else. Some time if that I send or write for you to follow me, do it swiftly as I may direct. Will you?"

I said yes with a sense that it was to one of my bringing up a little too romantic, and so far absurd; yet his tone was earnest, and even sad, and I therefore took care not to smile.

"That is all," he returned; and we went in.

All that time is broken up for me into distinct scenes like a play, some of them, as I said before, having the clearness of pictures, being like these but the scenes of a moment. The days and hours between are less well defined in my memory. There is one of these brief pictures which hangs as it were in my mind, and which I could wish that some one would paint for me.

The next day was Sunday, and Wholesome, as had often chanced of late, did not go to meeting, but after breakfast walked out of the room with a sombre face and clouded brow, and went slowly up-stairs to his chambers in the third story. In one he slept; the other was a sitting-room, filled with relics of his many voyages,—skins of wild beasts, deer and moose horns, pipes and the like,—of which I found it pleasant to hear him chat. I followed him up-stairs, and with Schmidt came to the door of his room, meaning to ask him to walk with us. He must have been much taken up with his own thoughts, for he did not hear us, and, the door being ajar, Schmidt of a sudden checked me and pointed into the room. Against the farther wall was a tall mahogany clock, such as are common in old houses here,—a rather stately timepiece, crowned with a carven cock over its ample metal face. Below it, on the floor, lay a large tiger-skin, upon which stood Wholesome. The clock-door was open, and he seemed to have just taken from its interior a pair of rapiers. One he had set against the clock, and unsheathing the other he held the point in one hand and the haft in the other, and bent it as if to try its temper. I can see the man now in his drab clothes, his curly hair, his look of easy, ample strength, the tiger-skin and the open clock. Then I can see him throw his chest out and lunge twice or thrice at the wall with the lightsome grace of a practised hand.

Schmidt stepped back on tiptoe, whispering, "Come

away," and silently we went down the staircase, I wondering, and he moody and abstracted, making no reply to my questionings and comments.

At last he said, "I walk not to-day. Will you please me to not forget what you have promised yesterday?"

The summons came soon. I was lying on the grass under the apricots, teasing the cat for the lack of better amusement, that Sunday in the early afternoon. Across me fell the shadow of Schmidt coming noiseless over the sward. I rolled over on my back, laughing and tossing the angry cat about, knowing not it was the shadow of a tragedy which had fallen across me at my careless play.

Schmidt regarded me a moment with a soft, grave look, and then, dropping on the grass beside me, said, "I have before me in the day which goes a business which will not be the play of boys; but being, as you know, a man of lonely ways, there is not one I can think to ask that they go with me."

"And why not take me," I said, "as you meant to do, I suppose?"

"I would not if I could help it," he returned.

"Now, Mr. Schmidt," said I, abruptly, "it is a fancy you and Mr. Wholesome have to make a boy of me; but if not forty, I am no more a boy than you. If you want help and I can give it, I am at your call. If you want to explain your purpose, I will listen. If you choose to hold your tongue, I am willing to go with you anywhere without question."

"That was nice-spoken," he said, quietly, "and with good trust. There will a woman love you well some day for the sweet honest ways of you. Come, then, and wait for me at the door a moment."

He presently appeared with a long plaid cloak over his shoulders, the air being shrewd and cool, and we went away down Arch Street together.

At the corner of High and Front stood a building with hipped roof and many gables, once the London Coffee-House, but at the time I speak of rather fallen in its fortunes to be a lodging-house of no great repute, but not ill kept, and in the war a great resort of privateersmen.

As we turned into the bar-room together, Schmidt said to me, "You are here only to see, and to remember what you come to see."

Then he exchanged a few words with the landlord, like himself a German, and, laughing gayly, went away up the narrow stairs to a front room on the second story, where he knocked. I heard no reply, but, at all events, Schmidt walked in, and as I passed him turned, locked the door, and, keeping the key in his hand, went a pace or two before me. At the table between the windows sat John Oldmixon. He turned his head, and with an oath too profane to repeat threw down his pen, and rising faced us. Schmidt walked to the table, and glancing at the half-written letter which lay there, said, smiling, "You write to Richard Wholesome? Then am I yet in good time."

"For what?" exclaimed Oldmixon, angrily. "To look at a private letter? Who the devil asked you to come here? Leave my room, or——"

"Hush!" said Schmidt, quietly. "You are, as I

do suppose, a man of the world, and what is called a gentleman. I have a brief business with you, which I would not for the sake of myself and you should be known."

"I do not know, sir," returned Oldmixon, "of any business you can possibly have with me. Open that door and leave my room."

"Ach! well!" said Schmidt. "Will you then listen to me?"

"No!" cried the other. "No man shall play this kind of game on me. Go, or I shall have to make you."

"It will be well if you shall hear me," replied Schmidt, quite master of himself.

"Then," said the other, "I shall open the door by force and have you put out."

"But to my side there are two," said Schmidt, as Oldmixon advanced.

On this hint I stood against the door, saying, "What Mr. Schmidt wants I know no more than you, but until you hear him you do not leave this room."

Oldmixon looked from one to the other, and then, as by a sudden resolution, said, "A deuced pretty business, indeed! I cannot fight two. What is it you want?"

"Now you are come into the land of reason," said the German. "I pray of you to hear me, and with tranquilness to think."

"Go on," said Oldmixon.

"Good!" returned Schmidt. "Mr. Wholesome,— who does well know all of you, from the one side of you to the other, what you call through and through, —he has his cause why he may not tell of you and send you away or have you put in jail."

"Nonsense! what stuff is this?" exclaimed Oldmixon.

"Yet hear," said Schmidt. "I have put on paper, which is in my pocket here, a little account of you for to be given to a magistrate. When he comes to see it there arrives straight the constable, and he touches you on the shoulder and says, 'You come with me.'"

"Pshaw!" said the other. "Is this a theatre?"

"It is a theatre," returned Schmidt, "and we are the actors, and the play is good. This paper you can have on your own terms if you are wise; and once it is yours, I swear to you I shall not ever in life speak or write of you again. But if you will not, then when I go from this, in a time but short, it shall be in the hands of the recorder."

"Do you take me for an idiot?" said the other. "What do I care for your terms? and what are you to me? Wholesome will never testify against me."

"Perhaps," said Schmidt; "and still you will be no less a man ruined; and here at least there shall be no place for you, and no woman—ay, not the lowest—will look on you with grace."

Oldmixon fell back a pace, hesitated, and said hoarsely, "What do you want?"

Schmidt leaned over and said something to him which I did not hear.

Oldmixon started. "Fight you!" he said, with a

sort of bewilderment. "What for? We have no quarrel. What utter nonsense!"

"Nonsense or not," cried Schmidt, "you fight or I go; and what shall follow I have not failed to tell you."

"Do you suppose," said the other, "I am to be at the beck and call of every foreign adventurer? If you come on Wholesome's quarrel, go back and tell him I will meet him anywhere with any weapons. With him, at least, I have a score to settle."

"And what score?" returned Schmidt.

"He has struck me," said Oldmixon. "I am only waiting my time. I have no quarrel with you."

"That is a thing easy to mend," said Schmidt; and to my surprise and horror he struck Oldmixon on the face with the leather glove he held.

The other, wild with rage, hit out at him fiercely as I threw myself between them, and there was a moment's struggle, when Schmidt exclaimed, stepping back, "Will that be enough?"

"Too much!" cried the other, furiously. "You shall have your way, and your blood be on your own head, not on mine. I take *you*, sir, to witness," he added, appealing to me, "that he provoked this quarrel."

"It is so," said Schmidt; and turning to me, "Let come what shall, Herr Shelburne, you will say it was my quarrel. And now," to Oldmixon, "the terms are but these;" and he talked apart with his foe a few moments. There was anger and dissent and insistance in their words, but I could not, and did not wish to, hear them.

At last Schmidt said aloud, "It is the letters against this paper, and Mr. Shelburne to hear and take notice."

I bowed, somewhat in the dark, I confess.

"Mr. Shelburne has my full confidence," said Oldmixon, saluting me, and now full master of himself. "And what time to-morrow shall it be?" he added.

"To-day," returned Schmidt.

"Ah! as you like," said the other, with a good show of indifference; "and the hour and place, if you please?"

"To-day," said Schmidt, "at six o'clock. There are certain willows of a clump which stand a mile below Passyunk Road in the meadow on the way to League Island. Four there are and one dead,—on the left. If at that hour we meet not, the word shall to the magistrate, as I have said it."

"Never fear," said Oldmixon; "I shall not fail you. The threat was little needed. Who is your second. Mine will be——"

"There will be no second or any to see," said Schmidt.

"But this is not a duel: it is murder!" exclaimed Oldmixon.

"We will call no names," replied the German. "Will you be there? And listen: if I am not of the lucky side, you will take this paper and your letters, and so will it end. That is my bargain, and you have much to win."

"Enough!" cried the other. "I shall be there,— ay, and ready. Your weapons?"

"These," said Schmidt; and throwing back his

cloak, he displayed the two rapiers we had seen Wholesome handling.

"At six?"

"At six," said the other; and with no more words we left the room.

During this singular scene I had held my peace, but as we reached the street I said, "You cannot mean to meet this man?"

"But I shall," he replied, "and you will here leave me."

"That," said I, "I shall not do. If you go alone, it must seem to any one a murder should either of you die. I go with you, come what may."

He reasoned with me in vain, and at last, seeing that the time sped away, he yielded, and we hastily took a chaise from a livery-stable, and, I driving, we went away to the place set. Within a hundred yards of it we tied the horse and silently walked down the road. Presently Schmidt got over a fence, and crossing a meadow paused under a group of pollard willows.

The scene is with me now, to fade only when I also vanish. A nearly level sun shot golden light across the tufted marsh-grasses of the low Neck lands, already touched with autumn grays. There was no house near us, and far away I could see over the ditches and above the dikes of this bit of Holland the tops of schooners on the distant Schuylkill. To the north the broken lines of the city still took the fading sun, while around us a chill October haze began to dim the farther meadows, and to hover in the corners of the dikes and over the wider ditches.

We had waited a few moments only, I leaning thoughtfully against a tree, Schmidt quietly walking to and fro, smoking as usual, and, as far as I could see, no more moved than if he were here to shoot for a wager. The next moment I started, as behind me broke out the loud roar of some ancient bullfrog. In fact, I was getting nervous and chilly. Schmidt laughed merrily at my scare. "And listen!" he said, as all around the frogs, big and little, broke into hoarse croakings and chirrups. "Ah!" he went on, "there is to nature always a chorus ready. Do you find a sadness in their tongues to-day?"

It seemed to me horrible, indeed, as I listened, but it had never so seemed to me before.

"And now is our man here," exclaimed Schmidt, as the sound of distant horse-hoofs caused us to turn toward the road.

A moment or two later, Oldmixon, who had dismounted and tied his horse, came swiftly over the field.

"There are two!" he exclaimed, abruptly.

"It is not my fault," said Schmidt. "But Mr. Shelburne shall walk a hundred yards away and wait. If you kill me, it will be not so bad a thing to have one to say there was a fair play."

"As you will," said the other; "but we did not so agree."

"The paper," said Schmidt, "is here; and the letters?——"

"Are here," returned Oldmixon.

"Mr. Shelburne shall take them, if you please," added Schmidt. "If you have good fortune, they both shall to you; and if I am to win, Mr. Shelburne shall me kindly give them, and I pledge my honor as a man to be truthful to what I have you promised. And as you are a gentleman, is this all of them?"

"On my honor," returned Oldmixon, proudly, with more courtesy than was common to him.

"These, then, to you, my Shelburne," said Schmidt; "and, as I have said, you will amuse yourself a hundred yards away, not looking until there is no more sound of swords."

I felt there was no more to be done, and so walked slowly away, carrying the papers, while the two men took off their coats. I turned at the sharp click of the meeting blades, and looked with wild eagerness. The contrast between the German's close-set, ungainly form and the well-knit, tall figure of his foe filled me on a sudden with foreboding. I was surprised, however, in a moment to see that Schmidt was a master of his weapon. For a minute or so—I cannot tell how long, it seemed to me an eternity—the swords flashed and met and quivered and seemed glued together, and then there were two cries of rage and joy. Schmidt's foot had slipped on the tufted sward, and Oldmixon's sword-point had entered his right breast. The German caught the blade with his left hand, and ran his foe furiously through the sword-arm, so that he dropped his weapon, staggered, slipped, and fell, while the German threw the blade far to the left. I ran forward at once.

"Back!" cried Schmidt; and, gathering himself up, said to Oldmixon, "Your life is mine. Keep still or I will kill you: as I live, I will kill you! You had Priscilla's letters: they are to me now. And do you give her up for always?"

"No," said Oldmixon.

"Then I shall kill you," said Schmidt. "Say your prayers: you have no more to live."

The fallen man was white with fear, and turned towards me for help. The German, hurt, unsteady, feeling his minutes precious, was yet cool and stern. "The words!" he said.

"I am in your power," said Oldmixon.

This was all, as it were, a moment's work, while I was advancing over the half-meadow across which I had retreated.

"Schmidt," I said, "for Heaven's sake, remember me at least. Don't kill a defenceless man in cold blood."

"Back!" he answered: "not a step more near or he dies as by you;" and his dripping sword-point flickered perilously over Oldmixon as he lay at his feet. "Quick!" he said. "I am hurt,—I fail. To kill you were more sure. Quick! the words! the words!"

"What words?" said Oldmixon. "I am in your power. What are your terms?"

"You will say," said Schmidt, his hand on his side and speaking hard, "you will say, 'I give back her words—with her letters.'"

"I do," said Oldmixon.

"And you hear?" said Schmidt to me coming near; "and take that other rapier, Shelburne."

Oldmixon had risen and stood facing us, silent, ghastly, an awful memory to this day as a baffled man, and around us the brown twilight, and his face black against the blue eastern sky.

"Yet a word more," said Schmidt. "You have lost, and I have won. To-night shall my charge be set before a magistrate. You have a horse: go! Let us see you not any more."

It was after dark by the time I reached home in the chaise with my companion, as to whom I felt the most bitter anxiety. At first I spoke to him of his condition, but upon his saying it hurt him to talk, I ceased to question him and hurried the horse over the broken road. When at last we were at our house-door, I helped him to get out, and saw him sway a moment as with weakness. As I opened the door I said, "Let me help you to bed."

He replied, "Yes, it were well;" and resting a hand on my shoulder, used one of the sheathed rapiers as a staff.

Candles were burning in the parlor, and an astral lamp, and voices sober or merry came through the half-closed door. On the hall-table was also a candle. Of a sudden Schmidt paused, and said in a voice broken by weakness, with a certain pitiful terror in its tones, "The power goes away from me. I grow blind, and shall—see—her—no—more."

Meanwhile he rocked to and fro, and then with a cry of "Priscilla!" he turned from my supporting shoulder, and as one dazed, pushed open the parlor door, and staggering, sword in hand, into the room, dropped it and leant both hands on the little round table for support, so that for a moment the light fell on his ghastly white face and yearning eyes. Then he swayed, tottered, and fell on the floor.

They were all around him in a moment with cries of dismay and pity.

"What is this?" said some one to me.

Priscilla was on the floor at once, and had lifted his head on to her knee.

"He is hurt," said I.

"Ah! God have pity on us!" exclaimed Wholesome, picking up his rapier. "I understand. Bring water, some one, and brandy. Quick!"

"Does thee see," cried Priscilla in sudden horror, "he is bleeding? Oh, cruel men!"

I stood by with fear, remorse, and sorrow in my heart. "It was——" I began.

"Hush!" broke in Wholesome, "another time. He is better. His eyes are open: he wants something. What is it, Heinrich?"

"Priscilla," he said.

"Priscilla is here, dear friend," she said quietly, bending over him.

"I thought I was a little boy and my head in my mother's lap. Where am I? Ah, but now I do remember. The letters!" and he fumbled at his pocket, and at last pulled them out. "With this on them," he said, "you cannot ever any more think of him."

They were stained with the blood from his wound.

"Never! never! never!" she cried piteously: "for this last wickedness no forgiveness!"

"And he is gone," he added. "And Shelburne,— where is my Shelburne?"

"Here! here!" I said.

"Tell her—he gives her up—for always—never no more to trouble her good sweetness. Wholesome, where art thou?"

"I am with you," said the captain, in a voice husky with emotion.

"Quick! listen!" continued Schmidt, gasping. "Time goes away for me. Is it that you do love her well?"

"Oh, my God!" said Wholesome.

"But never more so well as I," said Schmidt. "Priscilla!" As he spoke his eyes looked up with yearning into the face above his own. Then suddenly he drew a long breath, his hands ceased to clutch her dress, his head rolled over. He was dead.

When another summer again lit up the little garden with roses, and the apricot blossoms were as snow in the air of June, Priscilla married Richard Wholesome.

All of Heinrich Schmidt's little treasures were left to her, but out of his memory came to her other things: a yet more gracious tenderness in all her ways,—to her religion a greater breadth, to her thoughts of men a charity which grew sweeter as it grew larger, like her own spring roses.

The Quaker captain lived as he had lived, but grew more self-contained as years went by, and children came to chide with gentle wonder the rare outbreaks which were so sad a scandal to Friends.

We laid Heinrich Schmidt away in the shadow of Christ Church, and around his grave grew flowers in such glorious abundance as he would have loved, and by what gentle hands they were planted and cared for it were easy to guess.

I am an old man to-day, but I cannot yet trust myself to try and analyze this character of his. I still can only think with tenderness and wonder of its passionate love of nature, its unselfish nobleness, its lack of conscience, and its overflowing heart.

A DRAFT

ON

THE BANK OF SPAIN.

Not many of us would be eager to live our lives over again if the gift of a new life were possible; but when I think upon the goodness and grace and love that have these many years gone side by side with mine, I doubt a little as to how I should decide. Indeed, were God to give it me to turn anew the stained and dog-eared pages of the life-book, it would not be for the joy of labor, or to see again the marvels of growth in knowledge, that I should so yearn as for the great riches of love which have made for me its text and margins beautiful with the colors of heaven. And so, when I recall this life, and its sorrows and adventures and successes, with every memory comes to me first of all the tender commentary of that delightful face; and I rejoice with a sudden following of fear as I turn to see it again, and once more to wonder at the calm of sweet and thoughtful gravity which the generous years have added to its abundant wealth of motherly and gracious beauty.

It is a little story of this matron and myself which I find it pleasant to tell you; chiefly, I suppose, because it lets me talk of her and her ways and doings, —a very simple story, with nothing in the least startling or strange, but so cheerful and grateful to me to think over that I cannot but hope you too may get good cheer from it, and like her a little, and find interest in my old friend the clockmaker and his boy, and haply come at last to believe that you would be pleased to smoke a pipe with me, and to give me too of such love as you have to spare; which, I take it, is for a man to get from man or woman the most desirable of earthly things.

We had been married a twelvemonth, I think, and were coming on in years, she being eighteen, and I—well, somewhat older, of course. From among gentle and kindly folks, long and steadily rooted in the soil of one of our oldest Dutch towns in Middle Pennsylvania, we had come, with good courage and great store of hopes, to seek our fortunes in the Quaker City, whose overgrown-village ways always seem to the stranger from the country so much more homelike than the bullying bustle of its greater sister.

I smile now when I think what very young and trustful people we were, May and I, and how full of knowledge we thought ourselves of men and things. I had been bred an engineer, and when I married May was a draughtsman in a great manufactory, with just enough of an income to make our marriage what most folks would call unwise,—an opinion in which, perhaps, I might join them, were it not that so many of these reckless unions, in which there is only a great estate of love, have seemed to me in the end to turn out so well.

Away from broad fields, and laden barns, and my father's great farmhouse, and plenty, and space, we came to grope about for a home among strangers, with at least a hope that somewhere in the city we should find a little of what my wife's old father, the schoolmaster, used to call "homesomeness." With great comfort in our mutual love, we found for a long while no abiding-place which seemed to us pleasant, until at last a happy chance brought us to lodge within the walls which for some two years of our young married life were all to us that we could ask.

It chanced one day that I had to have a watch mended, and for this purpose walked into a shop in one of the older streets,—a place altogether deserted by the rich, and not fully seized upon by trade. There were many great warerooms and huge storehouses, with here and there between them an old house built of red and glazed black brick, with small windows full of little gnarled glasses, and above them a hipped roof. Some of these houses had at that time half doors, and on the lower half of one of these was leaning a man somewhat past middle life. The window-cases on either side were full of watches, and over them was a gilded quadrant and the name F. WILLOW. As I drew near, the owner—for he it was—let me in, and when I gave him my watch, took it without a word, pushed his large spectacles down over two great gray eyebrows on to eyes as gray, and began to open and pore over the timepiece in a rapt and musing way.

At last said I, "Well?"

"In a week," said he.

"A week!" said I; "but how am I to get on for a week without it?"

"Just so!" he returned. "Sit down while I look at it, or come back in half an hour."

"I will wait," said I.

Without further words he turned to his seat, screwed into his eye one of those queer black-rimmed lenses which clockmakers use, and began to peer into the works of my sick watch. In the mean while I amused myself by strolling between the little counters, and gravely studying the man and his belongings, for both were worthy of regard. A man of fifty-five, I should say,—upright, despite his trade,—gray of beard and head,—with an eagle nose and large white teeth. Altogether a face full of power, and, as I learned, of sweetness when I came to know better its rare smile. The head was carried proudly on a frame meant by Nature to have been the envy of an athlete, but now just touched with the sad shadows of fading strength. Wondering a little at the waste of such a frame in so petty a toil, I began to hear, as one does by degrees, the intrusive ticking of the many clocks and watches which surrounded me. First I heard a great tick, then a lesser, then by and by more ticks, so as at last quite to call my attention from their owner. There were many watches, and, if I remember well, at least a dozen clocks. In front of me was a huge old mahogany case, with a metal face, and a ruddy moon peering over it, while a shorter and more ancient time-piece with a solemn cluck, for which at last I waited nervously, was curious enough to make me look at it narrowly. On the top sat a neatly-carved figure of Time holding in both hands an hour-glass, through which the last grains were slowly dropping. Suddenly there was a whirring noise in the clock, and the figure grimly turned the hour-glass in its hands, so that it began to run again. The sand was full of bits of bright metal,—gold perhaps,—and the effect was pretty, although the figure, which was cleverly carved, had a quaint look of sadness, such as I could almost fancy growing deeper as he shifted the glass anew.

"He hath a weary time of it," said a full, strong voice, which startled me, who had not seen the clockmaker until, tall as his greatest clock, he stood beside me.

"I was thinking that, or some such like thought," said I, but feeling that the man spoke for himself as well as for his puppet. "I wonder does time seem longer to those who make and watch its measurers all day long?"

"My lad," said he, laying two large white hands on my shoulders with a grave smile and a look which somehow took away all offence from a movement so familiar as to seem odd in a stranger,—"my lad, I fancy most clockmakers are too busy with turning the dollar to care for or feel the moral of their ticking clocks." Then he paused and added sadly, "You are young to moralize about time, but were you lonely and friendless you would find strange company in the endless ticking of these companions of mine."

With a boy's freedom and sympathy I said quickly,

"But is any one—are you—*quite* lonely and friendless?"

"I did not say so," he returned, abruptly; but he added, looking around him, "I have certainly more clocks than friends."

"Well, after all," said I, "Mr. Willow, what is a clock but a friend, with the power to do you one service, and no more?"

"I think," said he, "I have seen friends who lacked even that virtue, but this special little friend of yours needs regulation; its conscience is bad. Perhaps you will be so kind as to call in a week; it will take fully that long."

I went out amused and pleased with the man's oddness, and feeling also the charm of a manner which I have never since seen equalled. As I passed the doorway I saw tacked to it a notice of rooms to let. I turned back. "You have rooms to let. Might I see them?"

"If it please you, yes," he said. "The paper has been up a year, and you are the first to ask about it. You will not wish to live long in this gloomy place, even," he added, "if I should want you."

Then he locked the shop-door and led me up a little side-stair to the second story, and into two rooms,—the one looking out on the street, and the other on a square bit of high-walled garden, so full of roses—for now it was June—that I quite wondered to find how beautiful it was, and how sweet was the breeze which sauntered in through the open casement.

"Pardon me," said I, "but did you plant all these?"

"Yes," he said. "My boy and I took up the pavement and put in some earth, and made them thrive, as," he added, "all things thrive for him,—pets or flowers, all alike."

I turned away, feeling how quaint and fresh to me was this life made up of clocks and roses. The rooms also pleased me, the rent being lower than we were paying; and so, after a glance at the furniture, which was old but neat, and observing the decent cleanliness of the place, I said, "Have you any other lodgers?"

"Two more clocks on the stairway," he replied, smiling.

"My wife won't mind them or their ticking," I said. "I am always away until afternoon, and perhaps she may find them companionable, as you do!"

"Wife!" he said, hastily. "I shall have to see her."

"All right!" said I.

"No children?" he added.

"No," said I.

"Humph! Perhaps I am sorry. They beat clocks all to pieces for company, as my boy says."

"Only my wife and I, sir. If you do not object, I will bring her to look at the rooms to-morrow."

As I turned to leave, I noticed over the chimney-place a tinted coat-of-arms, rather worn and shabby. Beneath it was the name "Tressilian," and above it hung a heavy sabre.

As I walked away I mused with a young man's sense of romance over the man and his trade, and the history which lay in his past life,—a history I never knew, but which to this day still excites my good wife's curiosity when we talk, as we often do, of the clocks and the roses.

I shall never forget the delight that my little lady found in our new home, to which we soon after moved. It was a warm summer afternoon, as I well remember. The watchmaker and his boy, whom I had not yet seen, were out, and the house was in charge of a stout colored dame, who was called Phœbe, and who was never without a "misery" in her head.

My May followed our trunks up-stairs, and went in and out, and wondered at the coat-of-arms and the sabre; and at last, seeing the roses, was down-stairs and out among them in a moment. I went after her, and saw, with the constant joy her pleasures bring to me, how she flitted like a bee to and fro, pausing to catch at each blossom a fresh perfume, and shaking the petals in a rosy rain behind her as her dress caught the brambles.

"May," said I at last, "you have demolished a thousand roses. What will their owner say? Look! there is Mr. Willow now."

Then, like a guilty thing, caught in her innocent mood of joy and mischief, she paused with glowing cheeks, and looked up at the window of our room, whence Mr. Willow was watching her, with the lad beside him. "Oh, what a scamp I am, Harry!" said she, and in a moment had plucked a moss-rose bud, and was away up-stairs with it.

When I reached the room she was making all sorts of little earnest excuses to the watchmaker. "But I have spoilt your rose-harvest," she said. "Will you let me give you this one?" and as I entered the man was bending down in a way which seemed to me gracious and even courtly, a moisture in his eyes as she laughingly pinned the bud to the lappel of his threadbare coat.

"Well, well!" he said. "It is many and many a day since a woman's hand did that for me. We must make you free of our roses,—that is, if Arthur likes."

The lad at this said gravely, "It would give me the greatest pleasure, madam."

I smiled, amused that the little woman should be called *madam* in such a reverential fashion, while she retreated a step to see the effect of her rose, and then would arrange it anew. They made freshness and beauty in the old wainscoted chamber,—the man, large and nobly built, with a look of tenderness and latent strength; the girl, full of simplicity and grace, hovering about him with mirthful brown eyes and changeful color; the lad, tall, manly, and grave, watching with great blue eyes, full of wonder and a boy's deep worship, her childlike coquetries and pretty ways. From that day forward father and son, like another person I know of, were her humble slaves, and from that day to this the wily little lady has only gone on adding to her list of willing vassals.

It was early agreed that the clockmaker, his son, and ourselves should take meals in common in our little back room, which, under my wife's hands, soon came to look cheerful enough. By and by she quietly took control of the housekeeping also, and with

Phœbe's aid surprised us with the ease in which we soon began to live. But as to the roses, if they had thriven in the care of Arthur and his father, they now rioted, if roses can riot, in luxury of growth over wall and trellis, and, despite unending daily tributes to make lovely our table and chamber, grew as if to get up to her window was their sole object in life. I have said those were happy days, and I doubt not that for others than ourselves they were also delightful. Often in the afternoon when coming back from my work, I would peep into the shop to see the watchmaker busy with his tools, the lad reading aloud, and my wife listening, seated with her needlework between the counters. Often I have stayed quiet a moment to hear them as the lad, perched on a high stool, would sit with a finger in his book, making shrewd comments full of a strange thoughtfulness, until the watchmaker, turning, would listen well pleased, or May would find her delight in urging the two to fierce battle of argument, her eyes twinkling with mischief as she set about giving some absurd decision, while the clocks big and little ticked solemnly, and the watches from far corners made faint echoes. Or perhaps, in the midst of their chat, all the clocks would begin to strike the hour, and on a sudden the watchmaker would start up from his seat and stride toward some delinquent a little late in its task, and savagely twist its entrails a bit, and then back to his seat, comforted for a time. My May had all sorts of queer beliefs about these clocks and their master, and delighted to push the hands a little back or forward, until poor Willow was in despair. One hapless bit of brass and iron, which was always five minutes late in striking, she called the foolish virgin, and at last carried off to her room, explaining that it was so nice to get up five minutes late, and the clock would help her to do it; with other such pleasant sillinesses as might have been looked for from a young person who kept company with idle roses and the like.

But if the clockmaker and my wife were good friends, the lad and she were sworn allies, and just the frank, wholesome friend she has since been to my boys she was then to young Willow. His white mice and the curiously tame little guinea pig, which had been taught not to gnaw the roses,—hard sentence for those cunning teeth of his!—were hers in a little while as much as the boy's, and the two had even come at last to share his favorite belief that the solemn old battered box-turtle in the garden had been marked with "G. W." by General Washington, and was to live to be the last veteran of '76. I used to propose in my unheroic moments that the old fellow should apply for a pension, but my jeers were received with patience, and this and other boy-beliefs rested unshaken.

There are many scenes of our quiet life of those days which are still present to me in such reality as if they were pictures which I had but to open a gallery door to see anew. The watchmaker seems to me always a foremost figure in my groups. He was a man often moody, and prone when at leisure to sit looking out from under his shaggy eyebrows into some far-away distance of time and space; almost haughty at times, and again so genial and sunshiny and full of good talk and quick-witted fancies that it was a never-ceasing wonder to us unmoody young folks how these human climates could change and shift so strangely. His wintry times were sadly frequent when, as we came to know him better, he ceased to make efforts to please, and yielded to the sway of his accustomed sadness. The boy made a curious contrast, and was so full of happy outbursts of spirits and mirth, so swiftly changing too, with an ever-brightening growth of mind, that beside his father no one could fail to think of him as of the healthful promise of the springtide hour. And as for my wife, in his better times the watchmaker had a pretty way of calling her "Summer," which by and by, for his own use, the lad made into "Mother Summer," until at length the little lady, well pleased with her nicknames, answered to them as readily as to her lawful titles.

I used to think our happiest days were the bright Sundays in the fall of the last year of our long stay with the Willows. We had taken up the habit of going to the Swedes' Church, which in fact was the nearest to our house, and surely of all the homes of prayer the quaintest and most ancient in the city. Always when the afternoon service was over we used to wander a little about the well-filled churchyard and read the inscription on Wilson's grave, and wonder, with our boy-friend, who knew well his story, if the many birds which haunted the place came here to do him honor. Pleasant it was also to make our way homeward among old houses long left by the rich, and at last to find ourselves sauntering slowly up the wharves, quietest of all the highways on Sunday, with their ships and steamers and laden market-boats jostling one another at their moorings, like boys at church, as if weary of the unaccustomed stillness. Then, when the day was over, we were in the habit of sitting in the open doorway of the shop watching the neatly-dressed Sunday folk, lulled by the quiet of the hour and the busy, monotonous ticking of the little army of clocks behind us, while my wife filled our pipes, and the talk, gay or grave, rose and fell.

On such an early October evening came to us the first break in the tranquil sameness of our lives. We had enjoyed the evening quiet, and had just left the garden and gone into the shop, where Mr. Willow had certain work to do, which perhaps was made lighter by our careless chat. By and by, as the night fell, one or two sea-captains called in with their chronometers, that they might be set in order by the clockmaker. Then the lad put up and barred the old-fashioned shutters, and coming back settled himself into a corner with a torn volume of "Gulliver's Travels," over which now and then he broke out into great joy of laughter, which was not to be stilled until he had read us a passage or two, whilst between-times my wife's knitting-needles clicked an irregular reply to the ticking clocks, and I sat musing and smoking, a little tired by a long day's work.

At last the watchmaker paused from his task and called us to look at it. It was some kind of registering instrument for the Coast Survey,—a patent on which he greatly prided himself. Seven or eight pendulums were arranged in such a manner that their number corrected the single error of each escapement. Further I do not remember, but only recall how we marvelled at the beautiful steadiness of the movement, and how my wife clapped her hands joyously at the happy end of so much toil and thought.

"It is done," said the watchmaker, rising. "Let us look how the night goes;" for it was a constant custom with him always before going to bed to stand at the door for a little while and look up at the heavens. He said it was to see what the weather would be, a matter in which he greatly concerned himself, keeping a pet thermometer in the garden, and noting day by day its eccentricities with an interest which no one but my wife ever made believe to share. I followed him to the open door, where he stood leaning against the side-post, looking steadily up at the sky. The air was crisp and cool, and overhead, thick as snow-flakes, the stars twinkled as if they were keeping time to the ticking clocks. Presently my wife came out, and laying a hand on his arm stood beside us and drank in the delicious calm of the autumn night, while the lad fidgeted under his elbow between them, and got his share of the starlight and the quiet.

"It seems hard to think they are all moving for ever and ever," said the boy. "I wonder if they are wound up as often as your clocks, father?"

"It is only a great clock, after all," said Willow, "and must stop some of these days, I suppose. Did ever you think of that, little Summer?"

"Will last our time," said my wife.

"Your time!" returned the clockmaker. "Your time is forever, little woman: you may live in the days not of this world to see the old wonder of it all fade out and perish."

Just then a man stopped in front of us and said, "Does Mr. Willow live here?"

"Yes," said I; and as he came toward us we naturally gave way, thinking him some belated customer, and he entered the lighted shop.

Then Willow turned again, and the two men came face to face. The stranger was a man of great height, but spare and delicate. He leaned on a gold-headed cane somewhat feebly, and seemed to me a person of great age. What struck me most, however, was the ease and grace of his bearing and a certain elegance of dress and manner. The moment Willow set eyes on him he staggered back, reeled a moment, and, catching at a chair, fell against the tall clock over which he had set the figure of Time. "What has brought you here?" he cried, hoarsely.

"My son, my boy," said the elder man, in a voice shaken by its passion of tenderness. "Can you never, never forget?"

"Forget!" said the other. "I had almost come to that, but, remembering anew, how can I ever forgive? Go!" he cried, fiercely, darting forward on a sudden and opening the door. "Go, before the madness comes upon me. Go, go before I curse you." Then he reeled again, and growing white, fell into a chair, and as if choked with emotion, stayed, rigidly pointing to the door.

Then my wife ran forward. "Leave us," she said, "whoever you are. You see how ill he is. You can do no good here. Come again if you will, but go away now."

The stranger hesitated and looked in bewilderment from one to another, while the lad, till then silent, opened the door wider and said, gently, "Will it please you to go, grandfather?"

"My boy—his boy!" exclaimed the new-comer, patting his curly head. "Now am I indeed punished," he added, for the lad shrunk back with a look of horror quite strange on a face so young, and, suddenly covering his face with both hands, the elder man went by him and passed out into the street without a word. Then the boy hastily shut the door, and we turned to Willow, who had fallen in something like a swoon from his chair. Silently or with whispers we gathered about him, while my wife brought a pillow and some water and gave him to drink. At last we got him up-stairs to our own room, where for some days he lay in a state of feebleness which seemed to me very strange in one so vigorous but a little while before. On the next morning after his attack he showed some uneasiness, and at length was able to bid us take down the painted arms over the fireplace and hide them away; but beyond this he gave no sign of what he had passed through, and by slow degrees got back again very nearly his wonted habits and mode of life.

I need scarcely say that so strange an event could hardly take place in our little household without awakening the curiosity of two people as young and romantic as May and I. Indeed, I greatly fear that the little lady so far yielded to the impulses of her sex as even to question young Willow in a roundabout way; but the lad was plainly enough schooled to silence, and you had only to look at his square, strongly-built chin to learn how hopeless it would be to urge him when once his mind was made up. He only smiled and put the question by as a man would have done, and before us at least neither father nor son spoke of it again during the next month.

The pleasant hazy November days came and went, and one evening on my return home I learned that Mr. Willow had suffered from a second attack of faintness, and from my wife I heard that the lad had let fall that his grandfather had called once more, and that the two men had had another brief and bitter meeting. The following morning, as I went to my work, I saw the stranger walking to and fro on the far side of the street. Nothing could be more pitiable than his whole look and bearing, because nothing is sadder to see than a man of gentle breeding so worn with some great sorrow as to have become shabby from mere neglect of himself. He peered across the street, looked up at the windows and at the shop, and at last walked feebly away, with now and then a wistful look back again,—such a look as I saw once in my life in the great eyes of a huge watch-dog whom we left on the prairie beside the lonely grave of his master.

From this time onward, all through a severe winter, he haunted the neighborhood, once again, and only once, venturing to speak to the clockmaker, to whom his constant presence where he could hardly fail to see him at times became a torture which was plainly wearing his life away. Twice also he spoke to the boy, and once urged him to take a little package which we supposed might have been money. At last my anxiety became so great that I spoke to him myself, but was met so coldly, although with much courtesy, that I felt little inclined to make the same attempt again.

I learned with no great trouble that he lived quietly during this winter at one of our greater hotels, that he seemed to be a man of ample means, and that his name was Tressilian, but beyond this I knew no more. He came, at last, to be a well-known figure in our neighborhood, as he wandered sadly about among rough porters and draymen and the busy bustle of trade. His visits to our house, and his questions about Mr. Willow, were added sources of annoyance to the latter, who rarely failed to look gloomily up and down the street, to make sure of his absence, before he ventured out of doors.

Under this system of watching and worry, Mr. Willow's attacks grew at last more frequent, and as the spring came on my good wife became, as she said, worked up to that degree that she at last made up her feminine mind; and so one fine morning sallied out and had her own talk with the cause of our troubles.

I think the good little woman had determined to try if she could reconcile the father and son. She came to me in the evening a good deal crestfallen, and with very little of the blessedness of the peacemaker in her face. While Mr. Willow was out she had sent his son, who was keeping guard in the shop, on an errand, and had then actually brought the stranger into the house, where, refusing to sit down, he had wandered to and fro, talking half coherently at times, and at last urging her to induce his son to speak with him once more. As to their cause of quarrel he was silent. "A lonely, sad old man," said my wife. He said he would kneel to his boy, if that would do good, but to go away, to go away and leave him, that he could not do,—that he would not do. God would bless her, he was sure; and might he kiss her hand? and so went away at last sorrow-stricken, but wilful to keep to his purpose.

Perhaps my wife's talk may have had its effect, because for a month or two he was absent. Then he came and asked at the door for Willow, who was out, and for a while haunted the street, until late in the spring, when we saw him no longer.

Meanwhile, Willow had become more feeble, and a new trouble had come to our own modest door.

Many years have since gone by, and happier fortunes have been ours,—brave sons and fair daughters, and more of this world's gear than perhaps is good for us to leave them,—but to this day I remember with discomfort that luckless evening. I hastened home with the news to my wife; and what news to two trustful young folks, who had married against the will of their elders, and had seen, as yet, no cause to regret their waywardness!

"May," said I,—and I can recall how full my

throat felt as I spoke,—" May, I—I am thrown out of work. The company is lessening its staff, and I am to be discharged."

I thought the little woman would have been crushed, but, on the contrary, it was I, who meant to comfort her, who was the beaten one.

"Well, Harry," said she, in a cheery way, "I did not suppose it would last forever."

Man though I was, I sat down and covered my face with my hands. We were very young, and very, very poor. I had been offered, not long before, a place in the West, but our little treasury was very low, and to secure the position with a probable future of success required some hundreds of dollars, so that we had not dared to give it another thought; and now, at last, what were we to do?

"Do!" said May. "Why—— But kiss me, Harry,—you haven't kissed me since you came in."

I kissed her, rather dolefully I fear. "We can't live on kisses," said I.

"Not as a steady diet," she replied, laughing. "Perhaps this may have good news for us;" and so saying, she handed me a letter.

I opened it absently and glanced over it in haste. "Misfortunes never come single, May," said I.

"No, my darling," she answered, laughing; "they only come to married people, to make them good girls and boys, I suppose. What is it, you grumpy old man?"

I read it aloud. It was a request—and a rather crusty one too—from a bachelor cousin to return to him a small sum which he had lent us when we were married. He had met with certain losses which made it needful that he should be repaid at once.

"Any more letters, May?" said I, ruefully.

"Nonsense!" said she. "Let us think about it to-morrow."

"What good will sleeping on it do?" I replied. "Do you expect to dream a fortune?"

"I have dreamed a good many," she said, "in my time, and all for you, you ungrateful fellow. Now suppose——"

"Well, suppose what?" said I, crossly.

"Suppose," she returned,—" suppose we two laugh a little."

That woman would have laughed at anything or with anybody.

"I can't laugh, May," said I. "We are in a rather serious scrape, I assure you."

"Scrape!" said she. "Old age is a scrape, but at twenty-two all the good things of time are before us; and—and God, my darling, has he not been very, very good to us two sparrows?"

"But, May," said I, "it is not myself I think of; it is——"

"Me, I suppose,—me. Do you know how rich I am, Harry? It seems to me I never can be poor. There's, first, your love,—that is twenty thousand dollars; then there is that dear old bearded face of yours,—that is ten thousand more; then there is all the rest of you,—that's ever so much more; and then there are my Spanish castles——"

"May, May," said I, "if castles in Spain would

aid us, I would gladly enough help you to build them; but for my part——"

"For my part," she broke in, "castles in Spain do help me. They help me to get over the shock of this horrid bother, and to gain a little time to steady myself. Indeed, I think if I were to draw a big check on the Rothschilds at this very moment, it would ease me a bit. It would ease me, you see, even if they did not pay it."

"May, May!" said I, reproachfully.

"Now, Harry," she cried, laughing, "I must laugh and have my nonsense out. I can't cry, even for you. Let us go out and have a good long walk, and to-morrow talk over this trouble. We shall live to smile at the fuss we have made about it. So, change your coat and come with me; I was just dressed to go out to meet you."

"Well, May," I said, "if only——"

"If!—fiddlesticks!" she cried, putting her hand over my mouth and pushing me away. "Hurry, or we shall be late."

I don't often resist the little lady, and so I went as she bid me, and by and by coming back, there was May laughing and making absurdly merry over a bit of paper on the desk before her. I leaned over her shoulder and said, "What is it, sweetheart?"

"Riches," said she.

"Nonsense!" said I.

"What a relapse!" cried the wifey. "So you despise gold, do you? See what I have been doing for you while you have been idling in the next room."

"What is it?" said I, laughing, for not to laugh when she laughed was simply out of the question.

She gave me the paper, and I read just this pretty stuff:

"The Bank of Spain, please pay to Bearer (who, the benevolent bank should know, is out of place and out of humor, and owes money not of Spain) One Thousand Dollars.

"$1000. "The Best of Wives."

We left the order and the wretched letter on the desk, and went merrily down-stairs, full once more of hope and faith, comforted somehow by so little a thing as this jest of hers. I made, as I remember, a feeble effort to plunge anew into my griefs, but May rattled on so cheerfully, and the laugh and the smile were so honest and wholesome, that good humor could no more fail to grow in their company than a rose refuse to prosper in the warm sweet suns of June. I have loved that woman long, and have greatly loved her afresh for the good and tender things I have seen her do, but it was on the summer evening of our trouble I first learned that I could love her more, and that truly to love is but to grow in all knowledge of such courage and winning sweetness and gallant, cheery endurance as she showed me then, just as it were for a little glimpse of the gracious largeness of this amazing blessing which had fallen into my poor lap and life.

That warm June afternoon was filled full for me of those delightful pictures which I told you have hung, with others more or less faded, in the great gallery of art which adorns my Spanish castle. There are bits by a rare artist of the long-gone gables and hip-roofs and half doors which used to make old Swanson Street picturesque. There is one little group of boys just loosed from school, ruddy and jolly, around a peanut-stand, alike eager and penniless, while behind them May—reckless, imprudent May!—is holding up a dime to the old woman, and laughing at the greedy joy that is coming on a sudden over the urchins' faces as the nuts become a possible possession.

We were great walkers in those days; and as we walked and the houses and poor suburbs were left behind, and we gained the open roads which run wildly crooked across the Neck, it was pleasant to feel that we had escaped from the tyranny of right angles. It was the first time we had gone south of the city, and we found there, as you may find to-day, the only landscape near us which has in it something quite its own, and which is not elsewhere to be seen near to any great city in all our broad country. It has helped me to one or two landscapes by Dutch artists, which will fetch a great price if ever my heirs shall sell the Spanish castle.

Wide, level, grassy meadows, bounded by two noble rivers, kept back by miles of dikes; formal little canals, which replace the fences and leave an open view of lowing cattle; long lines of tufted pollard willows, shock-headed, sturdy fellows; and here and there a low-walled cottage, with gleaming milk-cans on the whitewashed garden palings; and, between, glimpses of red poppies, tulips, and the like, while far away in the distance tall snowy sails of hidden hulks of ships and schooners move slowly to and fro upon the unseen rivers.

Charming we found it, with a lowland beauty all its own, lacking but a wind-mill here and there to make it perfect of its kind. Along its heaped-up roads we wandered all that summer afternoon, until the level sun gleamed yellow on the long wayside ditches, with their armies of cat-tails and spatter-docks and tiny duckweed; and at last the frogs came out, both big and small, and said or sung odd bits of half-human language, which it pleased the little woman to convert into absurd pieces of advice to doleful young folks such as we. She would have me pause and listen to one solemn old fellow who said, I am sure, "Good luck! good luck!" and to another sturdy brown-backed preacher, who bade us "Keep up! keep up!" with a grim solemness of purpose most comforting to hear. Then we stopped at a cottage and saw the cows milked, which seemed so like home that the tears came into my wife's eyes; and at last we had a bowl of sweet-smelling milk, and then turned homeward again, the smoke of my pipe curling upward in the still cool evening air.

It was long after dark when we reached home. As we went up the side stair which opened on the street by a door of its own, I put my head into the shop and bade Mr. Willow good-night. He was seated at his bench studying the strange swing of the many pendulums of his new instrument, but in place of the pleased look which the view of his completed task usually brought upon his face, it was sad and weary, and he merely turned his head a moment to answer my salute. On the stairs we met Phœbe, who was greatly troubled, and told us that a little while before dusk, Mr. Willow and his son being out, the stranger had called, and asking for my wife,— for the little lady, as he called her,—had pushed by the maid and gone up-stairs, saying that he would wait to see her. Phœbe, alarmed at his wild manner, had kept watch at our door until her master came back. Then she had heard in our room, where the son and father met, fierce and angry words, after which the old man had gone away and the clockmaker had retired to his shop. All that evening we sat in the darkness of our room alone, thinking it best not to disturb Mr. Willow and his lad, who were by themselves in the shop. About ten the boy came up, bade us a good-night, and soon after we ourselves went, somewhat tired, to bed.

The next day was Sunday, and as usual we slept rather later than common. After dressing I went into the back room, and, throwing up the window, stood still to breathe the freshness of the time. The pigeons were coquetting on the opposite gables and housetops, and below me, in the garden, the rare breezes which had lost their way in the city were swinging the roses and jessamines like censers, till their mingled odors made rich the morning air.

Suddenly I heard a cry of surprise, and turning, saw my May, prettier and fresher than any roses in her neat white morning-dress. Her face was full of wonder, and she held in her hands the papers we had left on the table the night before.

"What is it now, May?" said I.

"Look!" she said, holding up her draft on the Bank of Spain.

Beneath it was written, in a bold and flowing hand, "Paid by the Bank of Spain," and pinned fast to the paper was a bank-note for—I could hardly credit my eyes—one thousand dollars. We looked at one another for a moment, speechless. Then May burst into tears and laid her head on my shoulder. I cannot understand why she cried, but that was just what this odd little woman did. She cried and laughed by turns, and would not be stilled, saying, "Oh, Harry, don't you see I was right? God has been good to us this Sabbath morning."

At last I took her in my arms and tried to make her see that the money was not ours, but then the little lady was outraged. She called Phœbe, and questioned her and young Willow in vain. Neither knew anything of the matter, and my own notion as to its having been a freak of the English stranger she utterly refused to listen to.

It was vast wealth to us needy young people, this thousand dollars, and as it lay there on the table it seemed to me at times unreal, or as if it might be the dreamed fulfilment of a dream, soon to vanish and be gone. My wife must also have had some such fancy, for she was all the time running back and forward, now handling the note, and now turning to cry out her gratitude and thankfulness upon my breast.

To this day we know not whence it came, but as

Willow's father was plainly a man of wealth, and as he had spoken in words of strong feeling to my wife of the little service she had tried to render him, I came at last to believe that the gift was his. At all events, we heard no more of the giver, whoever he may have been. I trust that he has been the better and happier for all the kind and pleasant things my wife has said of him, and for the earnest prayers she said that night.

While we were still talking of the strange gift, young Willow suddenly returned, and, after waiting a moment, found a chance to tell us that his father's room was empty, and to ask if we knew where he could be. I felt at once a sense of alarm, and ran up-stairs and into Mr. Willow's chamber. The bed had not been slept in. Then I went hastily down to the shop, followed by my wife and the lad. On opening the door the first thing which struck me was that the clocks were silent, and I missed their accustomed ticking. This once for years they had not been wound up on Saturday night, as was the clockmaker's habit. I turned to his workbench. He was seated in front of it, his head on his hands, watching the pendulums of his machine, which were swinging merrily. "Mr. Willow," said I, placing a hand on his shoulder, "are you sick?" He made no answer.

"Why don't he speak?" said May, with a scared face.

"He will never speak again, my darling," I replied. "He is dead!"

I have little to add to this simple story. On inquiry I found that the stranger had left the city. No claimant came for our money, and so, after a little, having buried Mr. Willow in the Old Swedes' churchyard, we went away with his son to the West. The lad told us then that it was his father's desire that on his death he should take his true name. An evil fate went with it, and to-day young Tressilian lies in a soldier's nameless grave beneath the giant shadows of Lookout Mountain,—one more sweet and honest life given for the land he had learned to love and honor.

THE END.

www.ingramcontent.com/pod-product-compliance
Lightning Source LLC
Chambersburg PA
CBHW032129160426
43197CB00008B/570